Photographer's Guide to Polaroid Transfer

Christopher Grey

Amherst Media, inc. ■ Buffalo, NY

Published by:
Amherst Media, Inc.
P.O. Box 586
Buffalo, N.Y. 14226
Fax: 716-874-4508

Publisher: Craig Alesse
Senior Editor/Project Manager: Michelle Perkins
Assistant Editor: Matthew A. Kreib

ISBN: 0-936262-89-3
Library of Congress Card Catalog Number: 98-74541

Printed in the United States of America.
10 9 8 7 6 5 4 3 2 1

TABLE OF CONTENTS

CHAPTER 1
INTRODUCTION TO TRANSFER AND LIFT-OFF 5
• The Basics 5
CHAPTER 2
FILM AND RECEPTORS 8
• Polaroid Film Types 8
• Transfers in Color 9
• Color and Black & White Options 9
• Transfers in Black & White 10
• Receptors 11
CHAPTER 3
BASIC POLAROID IMAGE TRANSFER 13
• Wet Transfer 13
• Preparation of the Receptor 13
• Making the First Wet Transfer 15
CHAPTER 4
SPECIAL IMAGE TRANSFER TECHNIQUES 24
• Alternate #1 (Heated Receptor) 24
• Alternate #2 (Hair Dryer Method) 27
• Alternate #3 (Short Imbibe Time) 27
• Contributors to Quality 29
CHAPTER 5
DRY TRANSFERS 31
• Making the First Dry Transfer 31
CHAPTER 6
TRANSFERS WITH POLACOLOR PRO 100 MATERIAL 34
• Wet Transfers 34
• Alternate #1 (Hot Iron Process) 37
• Dry Transfers 42
CHAPTER 7
TIPS AND TRICKS FOR IMAGE TRANSFERS 45
• Borderless Prints 47
• Quick Dry 47
• Microwave for Effect 47
• Under/Over Exposure 47
• Pseudo Skin Tones 47
• Posterization 48
• Manipulate Colors 49
• Remove Emulsion 49
• Sandpaper and 8x10 Film 49
• Add Texture Under Transfer 49
• Add Texture Over Transfer 49

• Multiple Transfers (Small and Medium Format) 51
• Multiple Transfers (8x10 Material) 51
• Overlapping Transfers 52
• Add Color to Receptor 53
• Creative Vignettes and Break Lines 53

CHAPTER 8
EMULSION LIFT-OFF 57
• Materials Needed 57
• Emulsion Lift-off Procedure 58

CHAPTER 9
TIPS AND TRICKS FOR EMULSION LIFT-OFF 67
• Lift-offs and Other Surfaces 67
• Wax Paper Alternative 67
• Overall Color 67
• Cutting and Repositioning onto Colored Backgrounds 67
• Outline Images 68
• Problems with Close Dated Film 69
• Repair Small Holes 69
• Repair Large Holes 70
• Unique Corners 70
• Images Look Brighter 70
• Images for Transfer and Lift-off 70
• Mounting Multiple Images 71
• Mirror Images 71

CHAPTER 10
PRINTING TECHNIQUES 77
• Popular Printing Equipment 77
• Daylab II Slide Printer 77
• Daylab Junior 79
• Projection Printing in the Darkroom 83
• A Unique Trick for Projection Printing 85
• Live Transfers 85

CHAPTER 11
CARE AND KEEPING OF FINAL IMAGES 90

CHAPTER 12
WHAT'S NEW, WHAT'S NEXT 97
• Digital Technology 97
• Polaroid Negative 99

CHAPTER 13
FINDING MARKETS FOR YOUR WORK 100
• Editorial Markets 100
• Advertising/Commercial Photography 101
• Commercial and Personal Portraiture 101
• Weddings or Other Family Events 103
• Fine Art 103

CHAPTER 14:
AFTERWORD 105
INDEX 106

Chapter 1

INTRODUCTION TO TRANSFER AND LIFT-OFF

• THE BASICS

The principle behind the Polaroid Image Transfer process is extremely simple. A peel-apart Polaroid color film sheet is exposed. At a pre-determined point in its development cycle the material is pulled apart and the "print" portion is discarded. The "negative" portion is pressed onto a prepared non-photographic receiving surface and, when the remaining dyes transfer to that surface, a new positive is created. The resulting mixture of surface and chemistry give the positive its distinctive appearance *(fig. 1.1)*.

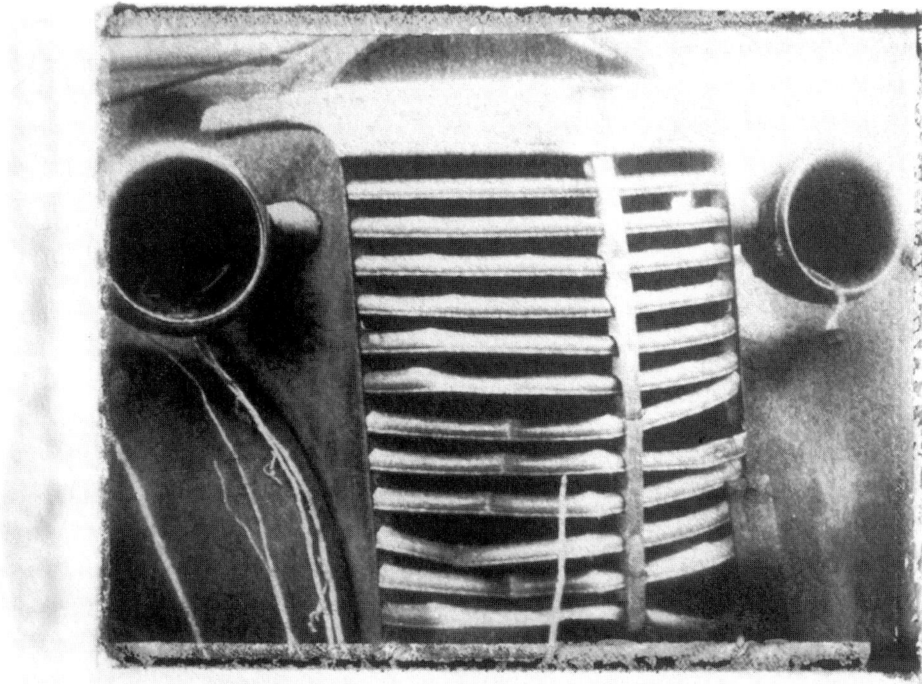

Fig. 1.1: *Use of a soft focus filter on the original slide gives this transfer a dreamier look than most. Type 669, Arches paper.*

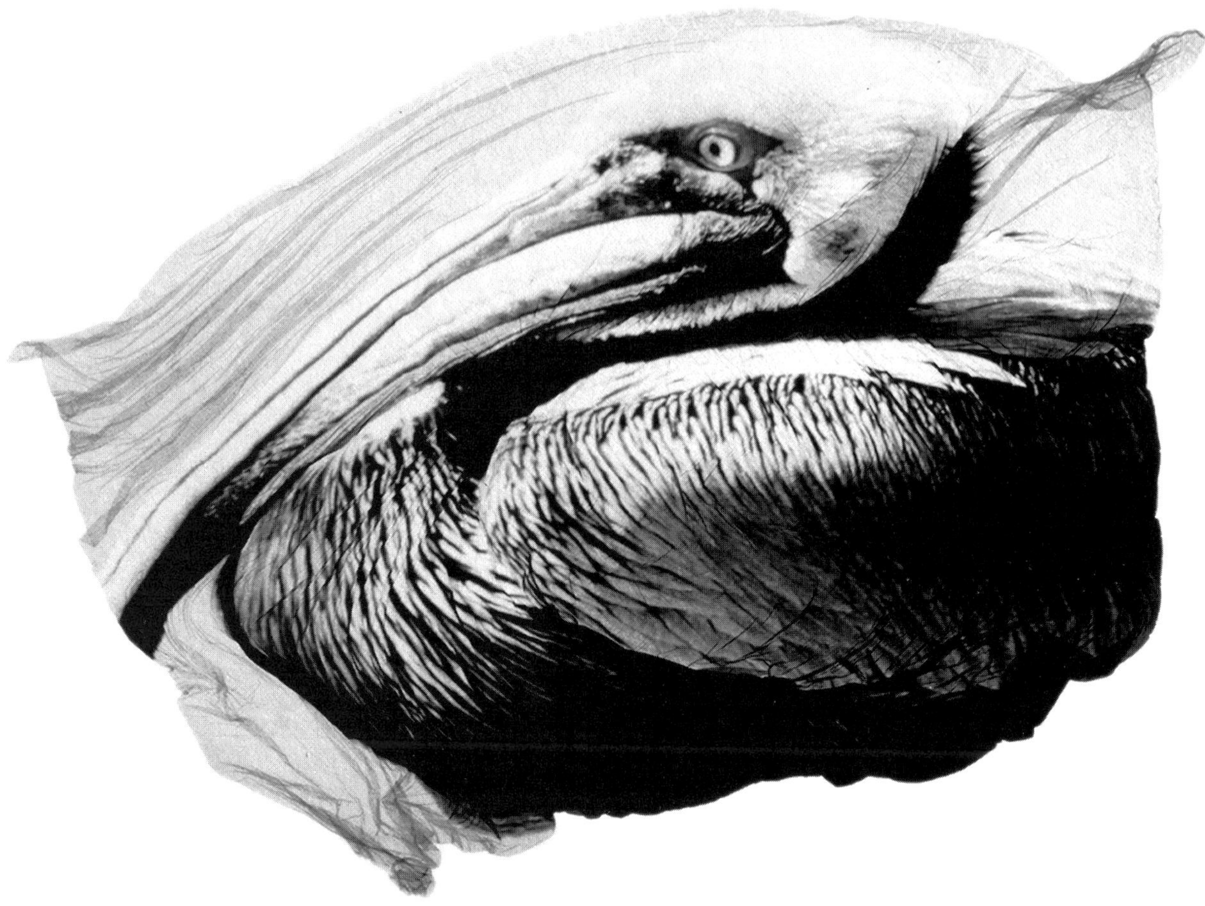

Fig. 1.2: *The fluidity of the loose emulsion makes it easy to mimic lines and shapes. Type 669, Arches paper.*

Emulsion Lift-off, in which the finished print is separated from its base and affixed to another surface, is also simple in theory. Soak a fully cured positive in hot water until the image can be floated away, then re-anchor it to a new base, the color and texture of which heightens the visual experience of the image itself *(fig. 1.2)*.

This book will explain basic techniques as well as special tricks to expand both of these Polaroid horizons. By themselves, the processes are nothing more than twists on instant imaging technology. In the hands of the inspired, however, the beauty found within a photographic oddity can create powerful and unique works of art.

Polaroid legend maintains that image transfer was accidentally discovered in the early 1960s when a Polaroid technician, testing yet another batch of the new peel-apart color chemistry, left a developed dye carrier (the "negative") face down on a white counter top. The next morning, irritation gave way to amazement and curiosity when the technician peeled the dry film from the surface and saw the test image had been transferred to the counter top as a positive.

Additional experiments were attempted, but actual progress with the technique was hampered when Dr. Edwin Land, Polaroid's founder and inventor of the instant process, insisted that such experiments were unnecessary and counterproductive. Polaroid consequently forgot about the process until professional photographers and other photographic artists, experimenting on their own, discovered it for themselves and began to ask questions that forced Polaroid to catch up.

I've tried every technique, trick and tip explained in this book. Most were discovered simply by asking "What If?" No matter how odd, I believe every idea is worth at least one piece of film. Each time I work with these techniques I'm challenged by beautiful, unpredictable processes that work in ways their developers could not have foreseen, and each time I realize how personally creative they are. You will too, from the moment you work with your first image.

Although it seems unlikely, it is possible to have "bad Polaroid days" in which only a small number of images come out the way you planned or hoped. This may be due to excessive humidity, lack of excessive humidity or possession by aliens. No one knows. Even though you may want to hang it up until another day, I would suggest you read the "special" text, as well as "Tricks and Tips" carefully. I believe I've made almost every mistake and had everything bad happen that possibly could. My solutions to common problems are found straight ahead.

QUICK REFERENCE:

Polaroid Transfer: The "negative" portion of an exposed Polaroid film sheet is transferred to a new surface by pressing it to that surface.

Emulsion Lift-off: The finished print is soaked in hot water to separate the image from its base. The image is the anchored to a new base.

Chapter 2
FILMS AND RECEPTORS

"Polaroid has several emulsion types and sizes available ..."

• POLAROID FILM TYPES

Polaroid has several emulsion types and sizes available for image transfers and emulsion lift-offs. Some, like professional Type 669, will do both. Other films, like those manufactured for Spectra, Sun and Captiva cameras, called "integrated" films, will not transfer or lift-off, although they may work nicely for other Polaroid techniques that require emulsion manipulation during image development.

The casual observer in any professional camera store would be surprised at the number of Polaroid films available, if that observer simply looked at the boxes. In actuality, Polaroid currently markets only four color emulsions (three balanced for daylight, one for tungsten), and the selections for transfer and lift-off are very simple:

FILM TYPE	SIZE	TRANSFER	LIFT-OFF
108	pack size	X	X
669	pack size	X	X
679 (Pro 100)	pack size	X	
689 (ProVivid)	pack size		X (difficult)
59	4x5	X	X
57	4x5 pack	X	X
64T	4x5 (tungsten balance)	X	X
79 (Pro 100)	4x5	X	
809	8x10	X	X

Polaroid peel-apart films were first introduced for the amateur market. Type 108 was the first general purpose color film produced in "pack" size, producing prints 3 1/4 x 4 1/4, eight per pack. The film was made for a number of cameras introduced in the mid-1960s and evolved for about twelve years. Faced with declining amateur sales, Polaroid began marketing to commercial photographers, shortly after which Polaroid made the jump from an amateur film to a professional one. Career photographers, always on the lookout for any way to pre-visualize the results of intricate lighting, exposure and compositional scenarios, found Polaroid emulsions to be a predictable and useful alternative to the nail biting and hair pulling that occurred while waiting for non-Polaroid films to be processed. Clients liked them too, for the same reasons.

It's still possible to find Polaroid Type 108 on store shelves, though the original emulsion formula has been discontinued for many years. Today's Type 108 is actually Professional Type 669 which didn't make the cut – an emulsion batch not quite up to pro standards. My experience with current Type 108 emulsions is that they are too warm (too red and yellow) to produce a neutral gray color. If packaged for professional use these emulsions would have been rejected, but for amateur use are better than one could expect from the old formula. The bottom line is that Type 108 is the same film as Professional Type 669 but is priced slightly less. It is also harder to find, since amateur Polaroid peel-apart pack cameras haven't been popular for many years and use today is limited to a small audience.

• Transfers in Color

Whether you work from existing originals or create one-of-a-kind images directly from the camera, all transfers or lift-offs begin with two-part, peel-apart Polaroid material.

"... work from existing originals or create one-of-a-kind images directly from the camera ..."

Most Polaroid material requires processing on the spot. If you're on location somewhere, and you wish to do wet transfers, you will not only need wet paper and a flat work surface but also a way to carry finished but still wet images out of the field when you're done. It is substantially easier to work from an original, positive image either in the darkroom or at a lighted work station to create your transfers.

• Color and Black & White Options

Black and white Polaroid material does not transfer or lift-off, but there are a number of ways to make black and white transfers using color film. I think those results are more spectacular than if it were possible the easy way, so we'll talk about that first.

• Transfers in Black and White

"... additional filtration may be necessary to get a more neutral gray on the final transfer."

Black and white Polaroid dyes, as found in Polaroid black and white peel-apart material, will not migrate to a receptor sheet, so transfers using such Polaroid material will not be successful. You must first make black and white prints and then copy those to a conventional color slide film, such as Ektachrome® or Fujichrome®, or to Polaroid Polapan® instant black and white positive film before completing the image transfer process. When making your own copies on a color slide film, additional filtration may be necessary to get a more neutral gray on the final transfer. I usually add a warming filter, such as a number 81C, to the camera. The end result, a warm-toned, monochromatic slide, looks great by itself but eliminates any of the cyan color shift that may be seen in Polaroid transfers *(fig 2.1)*.

Amateur color slide films, such as the basic Ektachrome emulsion sold in many discount and department stores, can be used, although the professional emulsions available in camera stores are manufactured to tighter tolerances. Amateur film emulsions are not consistent from batch to batch, but cost less than their professional counterparts. It's a good idea to test any film before buying more than a roll or two. If you find an emulsion batch you like (as distinguished by number on the film box), buy as much as you can afford. Unlike Polaroid film, traditional color slide films may be frozen until needed.

Copying black and whites onto Ektachrome through a deep sepia filter such as the Cokin Sepia can impart an antique feel to the final transfer or lift-off. Monochromatic effects from other filters or filter combinations can also be used to affect final color.

Copies made using Polapan black and white slide film frequently show a green/cyan color shift on final transfers and lift-offs, and it may be necessary to add substantial yellow, red or magenta filtration to counteract it.

We will use the Ektachrome color copy slide as the basis for our black and white transfers. When a monochromatic black and white image is re-exposed by the color printer, it gets the benefit of creation by four colors – yellow, magenta, cyan and black – instead of simple black dye only. Because it gets the benefit of colors not present in the original, grayscale version, the end result is an image with more visual depth and richness than one could ever get from black and white only.

• RECEPTORS

Most image transfers are made onto a presoaked, still wet surface. Almost any porous surface may be used, provided it is smooth enough to provide good contact with the negative.

"Most image transfers are made onto a presoaked, still wet surface."

You can narrow the odds for success by understanding some of the variables that contribute to good and bad results. You have the most control over the "receptor"– the surface that has been prepared, usually by soaking in water, to receive the Polaroid negative and allow the transfer to take place. Wet paper receptors are used for both transfer and lift-off procedures. Of those used, watercolor paper is the most common. Almost any watercolor paper will do,

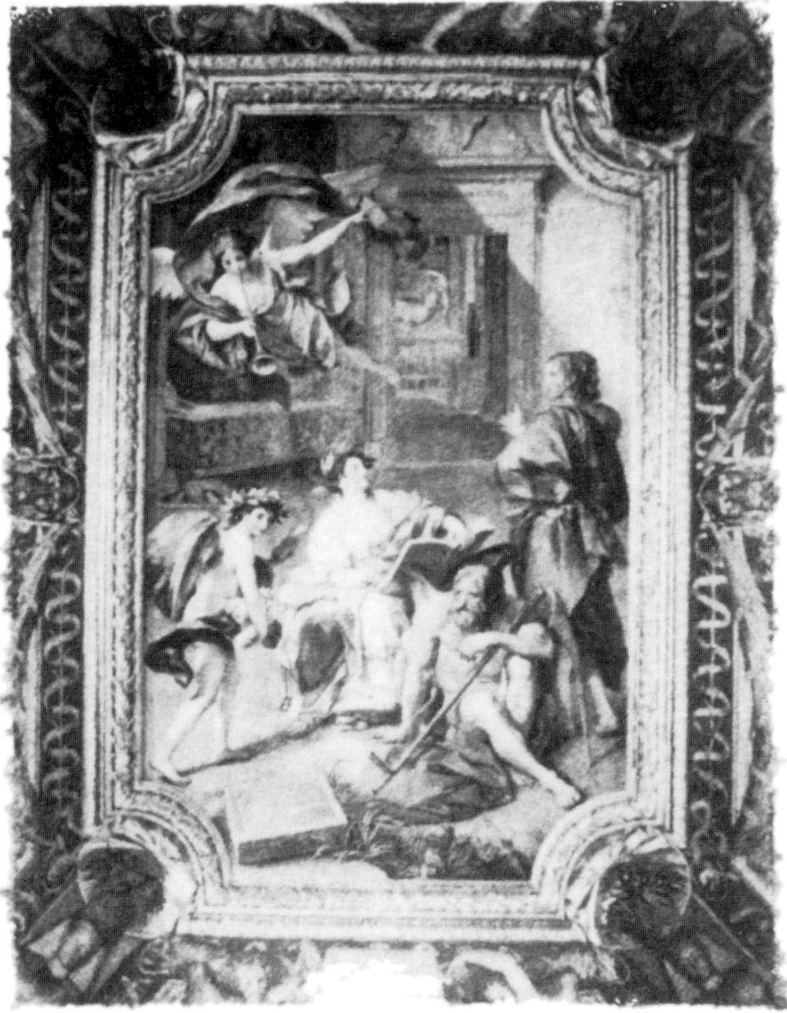

Fig. 2.1: *An example of detail achievable with Pro 100 film and Alternate Transfer Procedure #1. Type 679, Arches paper.*

QUICK REFERENCE:

Common Receptors for Polaroid Transfers:

- Watercolor paper
- Natural fiber cloth
- Unvarnished wood
- Plaster

Common Receptors for Emulsion Lift-offs:

- All of above, plus:
- Glass
- Metal
- Rock

but the most consistent is Arches 140# Hot Press, Smooth Surface. This paper has an ultra-fine weave that looks extremely smooth, yet has enough texture to grab the transferring dyes without blur or spread. The result is sharper images with well defined color boundaries.

Many other manufacturers make quality watercolor paper quite suitable for Polaroid transfer. Surface texture is very important to the quality of the finished transfer as well as an indicator of final transfer quality. With any surface, the key is to practice.

You may also use cloth. Natural fibers, such as 100% cotton, are best. Many synthetics are too stain resistant for dyes to penetrate and so do not work well. Any cloth should be washed to eliminate any starch that may have been put in by the manufacturer, then ironed smooth before use.

Unvarnished wood makes an excellent receptor for both transfers and lift-offs as the grain picks up nuance from the dye and adds dimension to the image. You may use any type of wood, although one of the easiest to obtain in a variety of thicknesses and surfaces is veneered plywood. Available in oak, birch and other surfaces, it is uniform in color and thickness and pre-sanded. Wood may be used wet or dry. For an even more individual look, scout local hardware "superstores" for wide rolls of exotic hardwood veneers.

Plaster slabs or sheets may also be used as receptors.

All of the above listed surfaces are also quite suitable, wet or dry, for emulsion lift-off. For lift-offs, harder, virtually impenetrable surfaces like rock, metal and glass may also be used.

Chapter 3

BASIC POLAROID IMAGE TRANSFER

• WET TRANSFER

There are many ways to produce a fine image, and we will examine some variations later, but this is what I would consider to be the basic technique to achieve a high quality, wet image transfer.

The materials needed for wet transfer are:

- Clean tray, slightly larger than your working paper size
- Watercolor or other receptor of choice
- Rubber or nylon "J-Roller" or brayer, 2" minimum, 4" maximum width
- Paper towels
- Disposable rubber surgical gloves
- Polaroid material of choice
- Correct equipment for chosen printing method.

Polaroid markets a Transfer Kit, available through many professional camera stores as well as Polaroid itself. For a reasonable price you will get a digital timer, high temperature thermometer, two plastic trays, soft rubber roller, rubber tong, sheets of watercolor paper and acetate as well as instructions for use. This is everything a beginner needs to do basic transfer and lift-off procedures.

QUICK TIPS:

There are two types of rollers, or brayers, commonly available. One is made of soft rubber, the other of hard nylon or acrylic plastic.

The soft rubber roller will generally produce a more finely detailed transfer than its harder acrylic counterpart. The soft rubber conforms to the material and the work surface more readily, and glides more evenly over the surface. This spreads the dyes smoothly but also pushes them into the pores of the paper.

By comparison, the hard rollers seem to "attack" the carrier surface. The end result is that dyes do not transfer as smoothly, and because it cannot smooth the dyes into the pores, the final texture has a rougher look.

• PREPARATION OF THE RECEPTOR

Wet transfers all begin by soaking the receptor (usually paper) in water until thoroughly wet, about ten minutes. Be sure to prepare the receptors at least that far in advance of your first exposure.

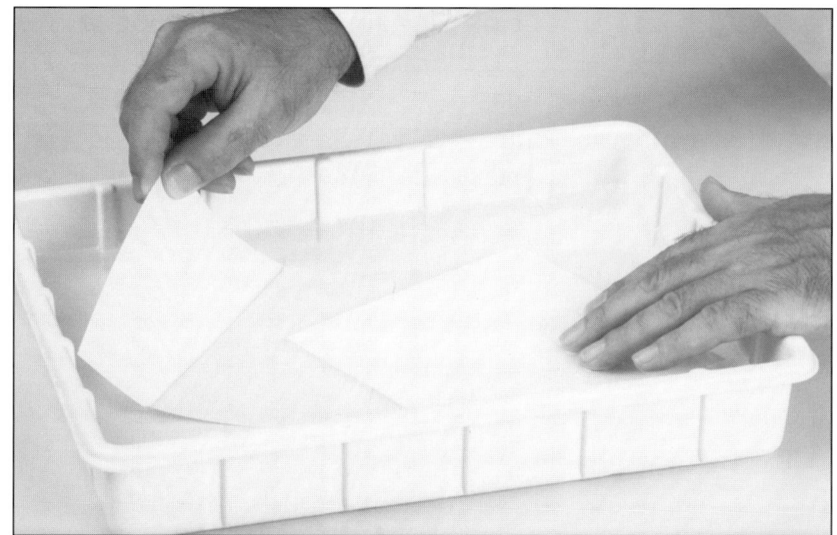

Fig. 3. 1: *Soak watercolor paper at least ten minutes and shuffle the sheets within the pile to insure uniform wetness.*

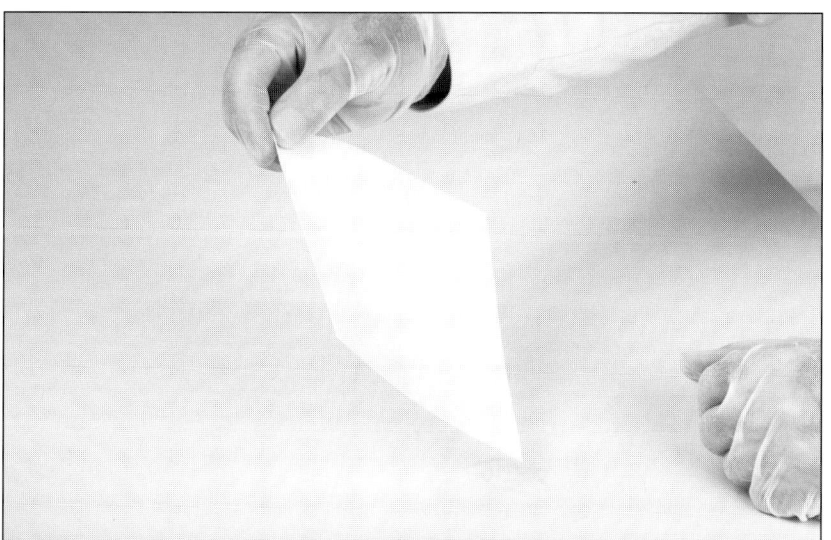

Fig. 3.2: *Drain five seconds and place on a smooth, waterproof surface.*

Begin by filling a clean tray, slightly larger than your working paper size, about half full with room temperature tap water *(fig. 3.1)*. If your water is excessively hard you may wish to use distilled water. Pre-cut your watercolor paper to a close approximate end size (you never get the Polaroid material lined up exactly right when its placed on the receptor, so you need to leave yourself room to trim down to final, edge parallel, size). Immerse the sheets into the soak tray one at a time and make certain each is thoroughly covered and slightly wet before adding the next, otherwise the sheet may stick to others and soak unevenly. For paper left in trays for a long time, sticking isn't a concern; eventually the water will soak through all the layers and the paper will be uniformly wet.

When you're ready for the first exposure, remove one sheet of wet paper from the tray, let it drip out for about five

QUICK TIPS:

With Arches, as well as some other papers, some discoloration will occur after prolonged immersion in water, usually in the form of small "dots" of mildew-like color, on the surface of the papers after immersion for more than fifteen minutes. They are not mildew, nor are they permanent. They will disappear without a trace after the paper has completely dried.

seconds, and lay it out on a clean, flat, waterproof surface like Formica® *(fig. 3.2)*. If a Formica-like surface is not available, a piece of Plexiglas® or other acrylic material, larger than the size of your receptor paper, will work over a non-waterproof surface, provided both surfaces are relatively flat.

Using paper towels and a not-too-heavy hand, soak up about 50% of the water using a side-to-side motion across the center of the paper *(fig. 3.3)*.

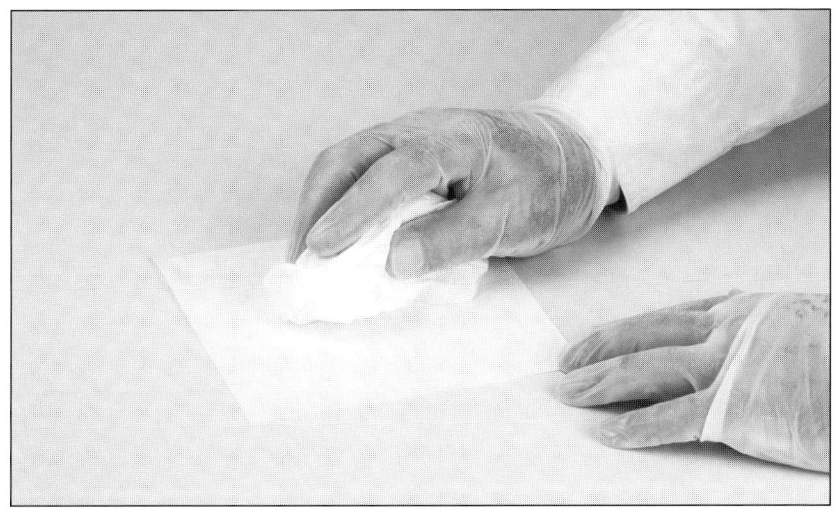

Fig. 3.3: *Wipe up approximately 50% of the remaining water with non-shredding towels.*

• MAKING THE FIRST WET TRANSFER: THE BASIC TECHNIQUE

Safety. Wear your gloves. Always. The chemistry is caustic, and you will most certainly come in contact with it. Repeated contact on unprotected skin can result in chemical burns or blisters. Read the cautionary notes enclosed with the material.

Imbibe Time. Make the first exposure, then pull the Polaroid through the processor. Watch the clock so you'll know when to pull the material apart.

Polaroid's recommendation is to wait ten seconds before peeling the material apart. This allows the dyes time to "imbibe," to mix together and begin the migration to the receptor. I personally like the results from a thirty second imbibe time much more than ten, and base the majority of my images on the longer time. At thirty seconds, the chemistry has mixed enough to transfer strong colors and a lot of detail. After thirty seconds, the longer you allow material to imbibe the lighter, more pastel your transfer colors will be. After sixty seconds, almost all chemistry will have been absorbed by the Polaroid receptor. The illustrations on the following pages may help you decide your preference *(figs. 3.5-3.15)*.

During the imbibe time, if you use Type 108 or 669 (or Type 809 for 8x10s) material, cut or tear the paper that attaches the negative carrier to the Polaroid receptor where the two pieces meet at the "tongue." If you use Type 59, 79 or 64T you might also cut the metal-encased chemical trap from the bottom – it will eliminate a lot of unnecessary chemical ooze and provide for a tighter bond to the paper at the end of the print. Some transfer enthusiasts leave it in place, preferring the slightly uneven look that results at the base of the print. Try both ways and make your own call. Either way, do not separate the receptor/carrier until the end of your selected imbibe time *(fig. 3.4)*.

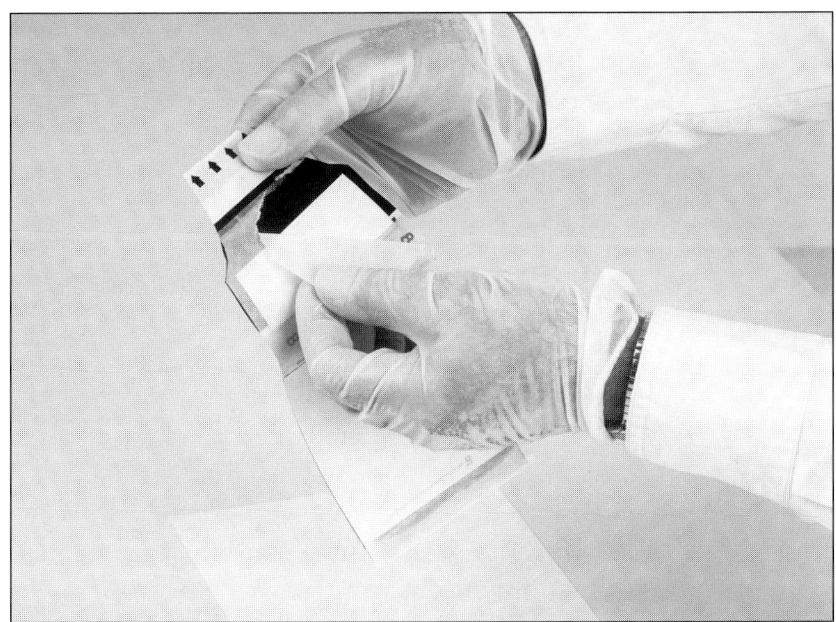

Fig. 3.4: *After the image has been pulled through the processor, break the paper seal between the layers. Peel apart at the end of the imbibe time and discard the positive.*

Making the Transfer. At the end of the imbibe time, pull the positive and negative pieces of Polaroid apart in one unhesitating motion and discard the positive print half. Take the dye-carrying negative half in both hands and place it face down on the wet receptor. It should take you approximately five seconds to complete this entire move. Once in place, don't let it slide around – the image will streak (unless you want that effect) *(fig. 3.16)*.

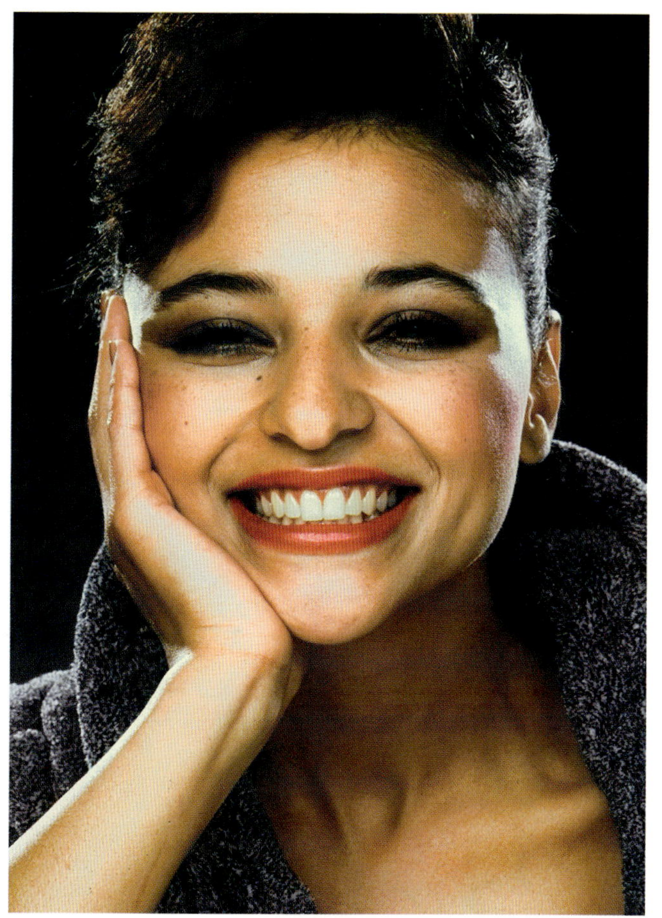

Fig. 3.5

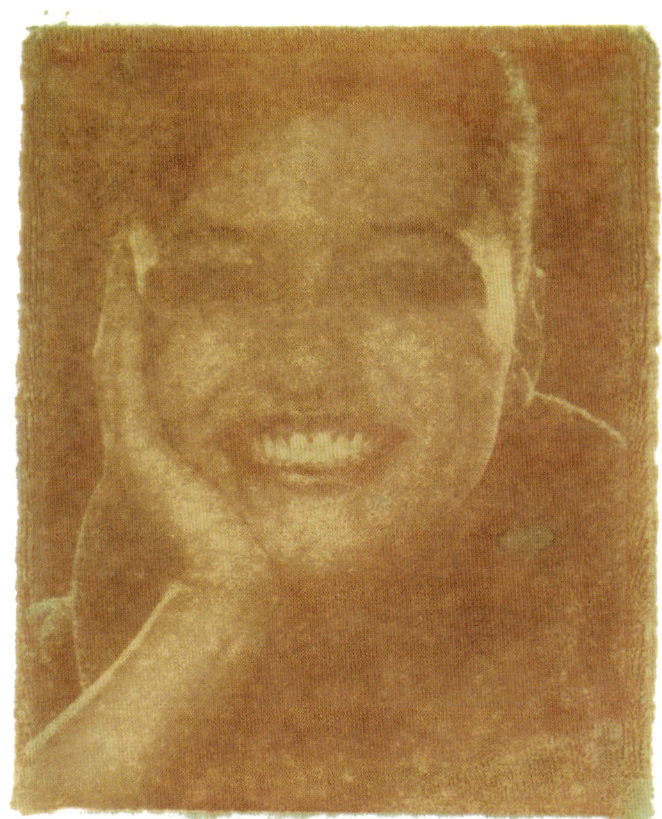

Fig. 3.6

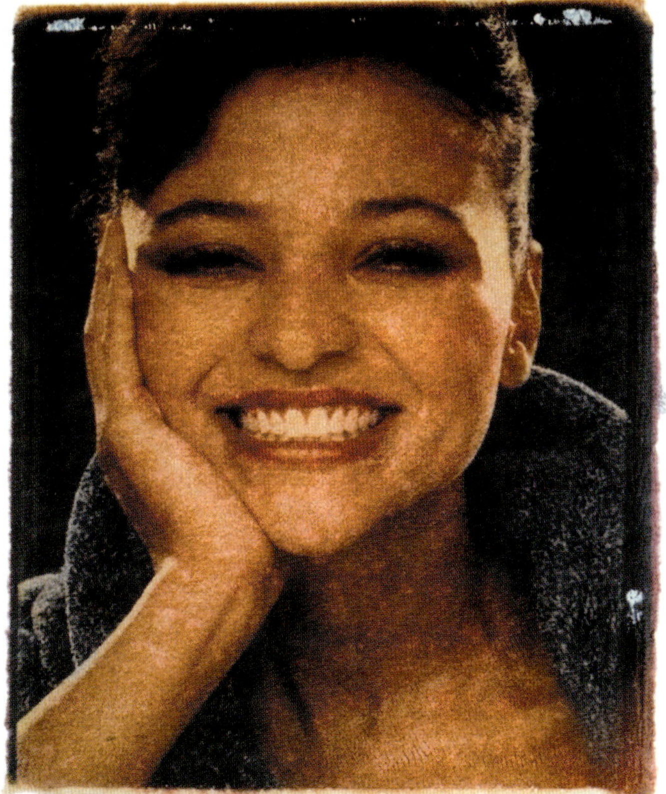

Fig. 3.7

Fig. 3.5: *Original image*
Fig. 3.6: *Normal exposure, five second imbibe time*
Fig. 3.7: *Normal exposure, ten second imbibe time*

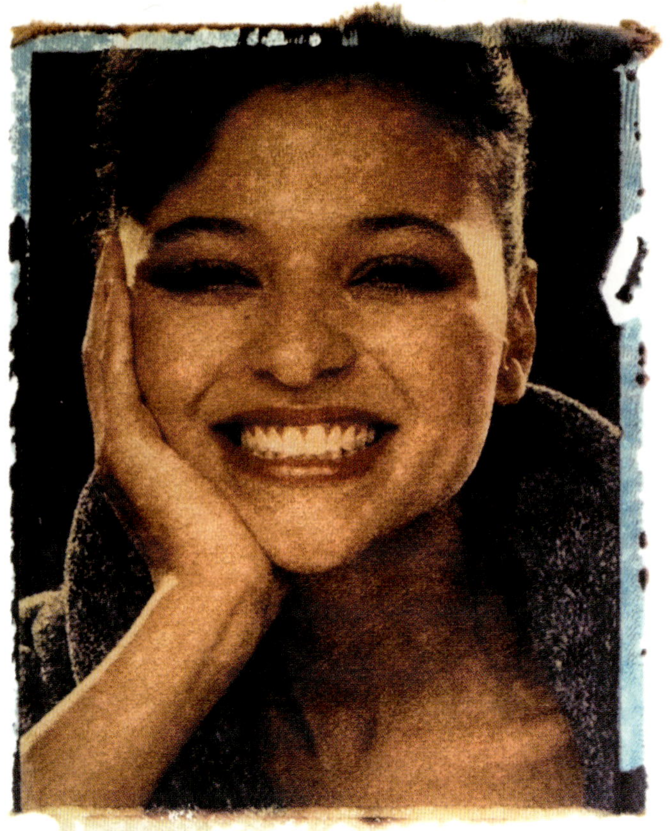

Fig. 3.8

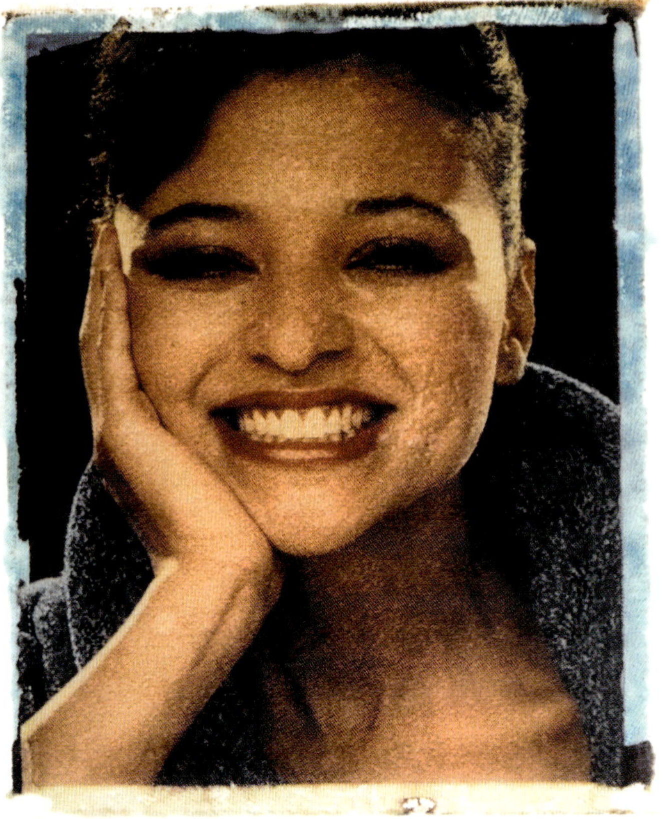

Fig. 3.9

Fig. 3.8: *Normal exposure, fifteen second imbibe time*

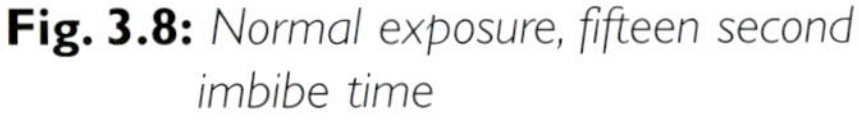

Fig. 3.9: *Normal exposure, twenty second imbibe time*

Fig. 3.10: *Normal exposure, twenty-five second imbibe time*

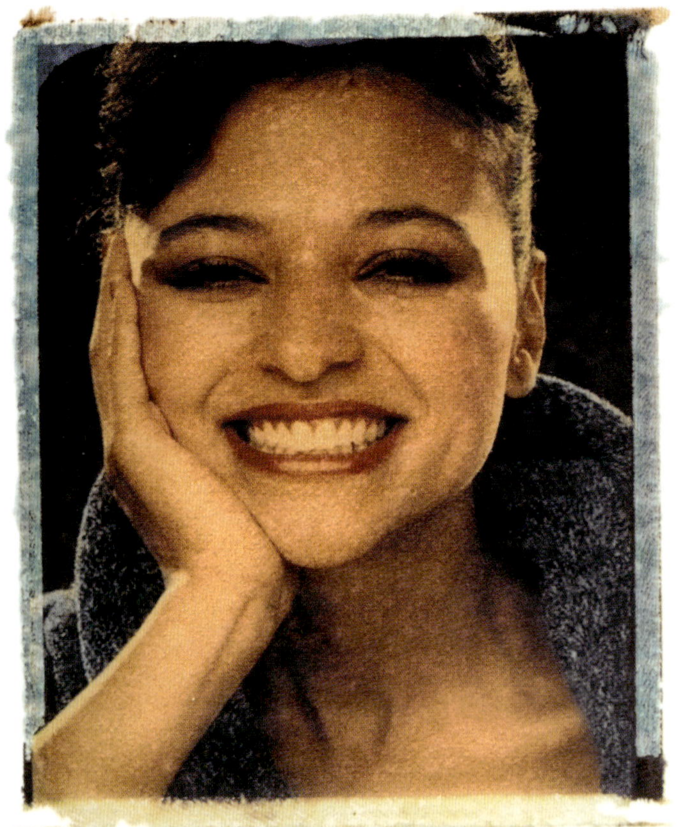

Fig. 3.10

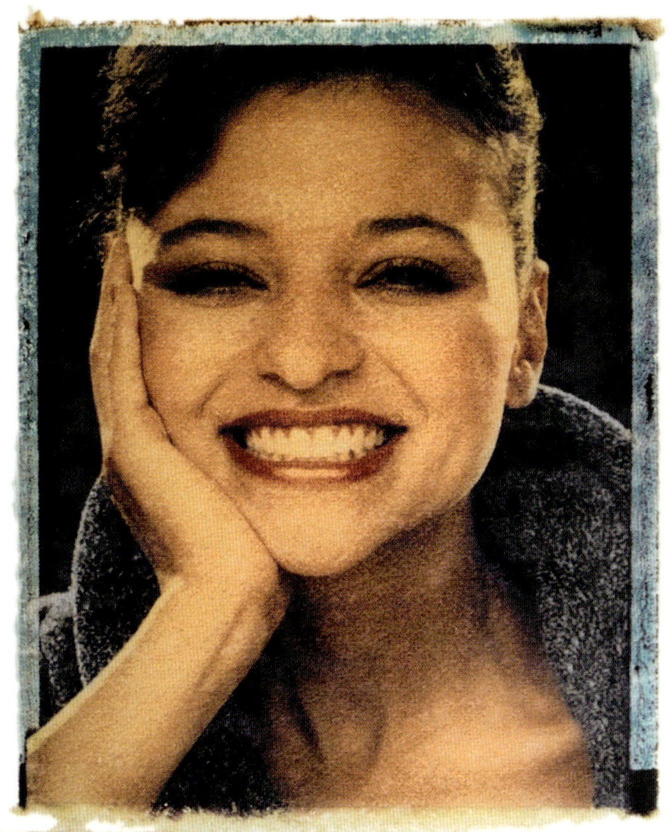

Fig. 3.11

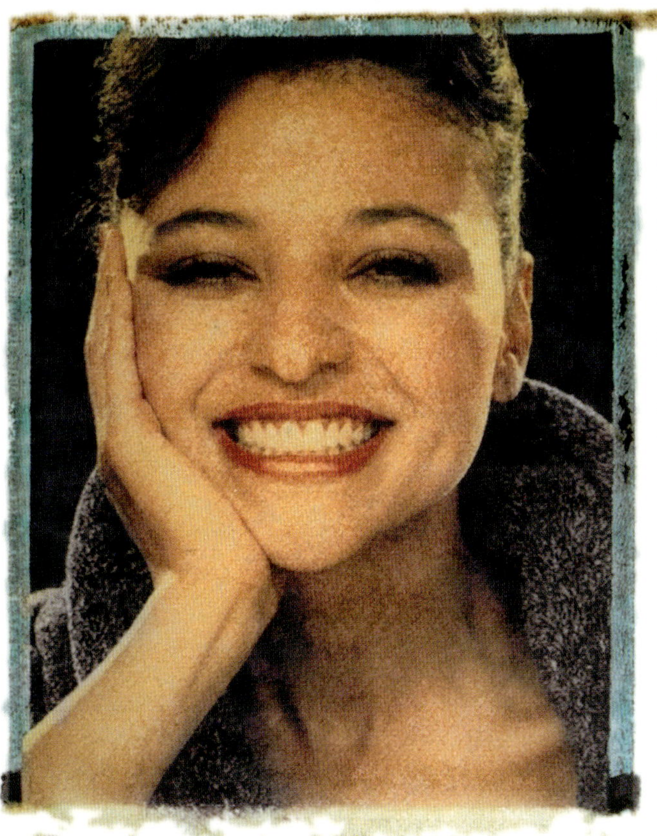

Fig. 3.12

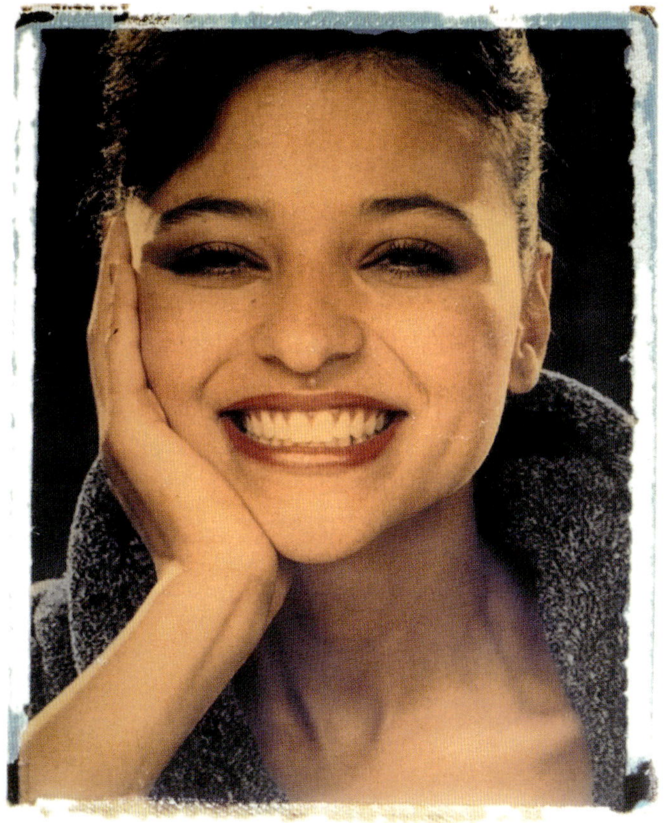

Fig. 3.13

Fig. 3.11: *Normal exposure, thirty second imbibe time*
Fig. 3.12: *Normal exposure, thirty second imbibe time, hard roller*
Fig. 3.13: *Normal exposure, thirty second imbibe time, dry transfer, soft rubber roller*

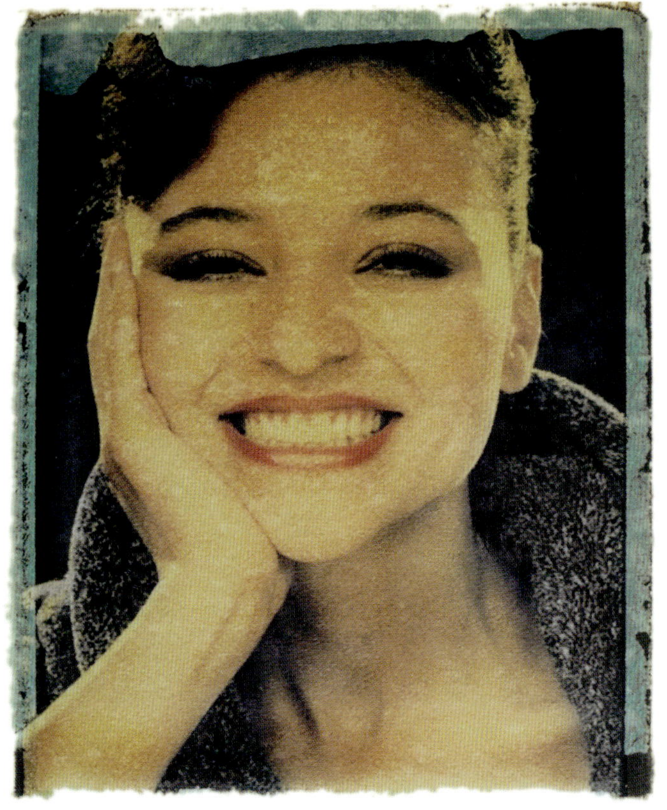

Fig. 3.14

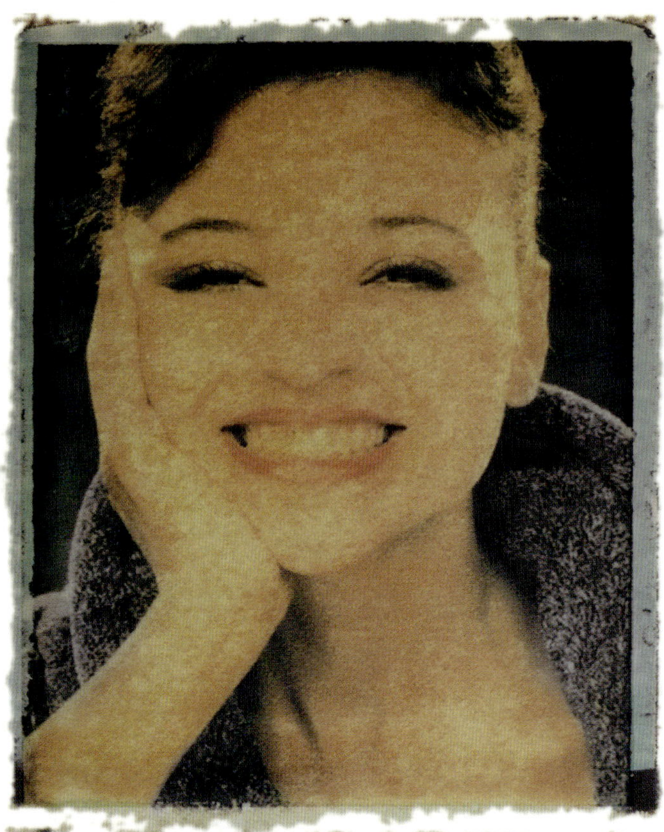

Fig. 3.15

Fig. 3.14: *Normal exposure, forty-five second imbibe time*
Fig. 3.15: *Normal exposure, sixty second imbibe time*

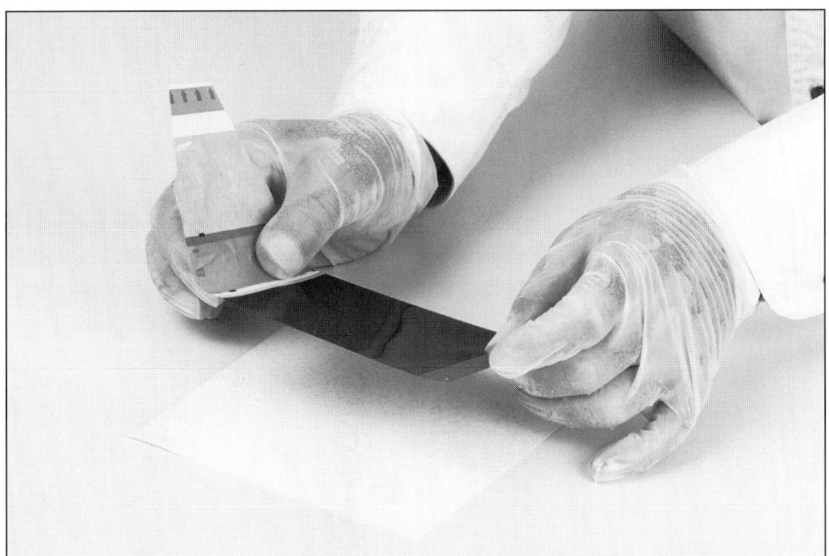

Fig. 3.16: *Hold carrier with both hands and place face down on paper.*

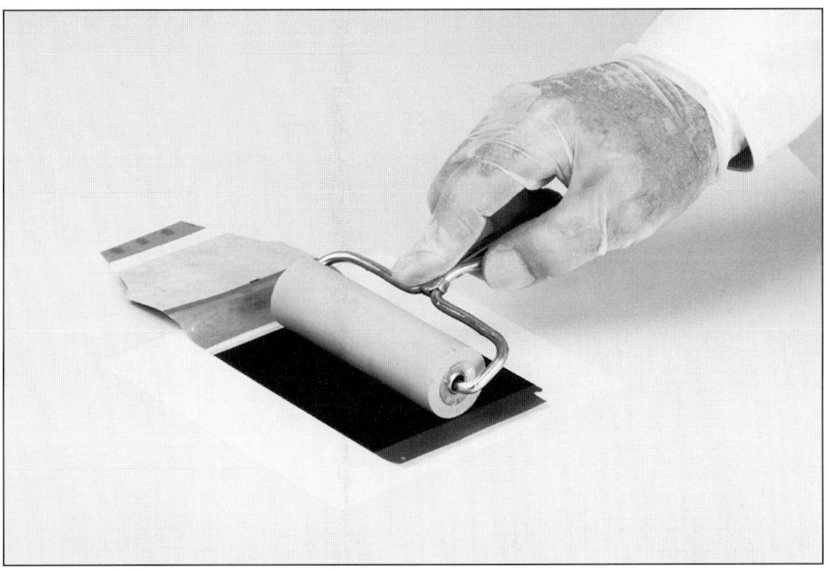

Fig. 3.17: *Using selected brayer, roll in both directions for two minutes. Use moderate pressure.*

Immediately after laying the dye carrier onto the receptor, use the brayer and roll the dye into the paper *(fig. 3.17)*. Roll in all directions, but avoid rolling chemistry out of the end of the material. In other words, if the dyes bubble out from under the sides of the carrier you're probably rolling too hard. Roll back and forth against the back of the carrier surface for two minutes.

After two minutes you're ready to peel the carrier from your first transfer *(fig. 3.18)*.

Without lifting the receptor (the positive) from the work surface, lift the carrier material (the negative) by the long tab and, holding that tab bent over almost parallel to the paper, break the carrier's bond to the watercolor paper. Bending the tab at an angle so as to break the bond at a corner usually works best. Pull the carrier back over itself until

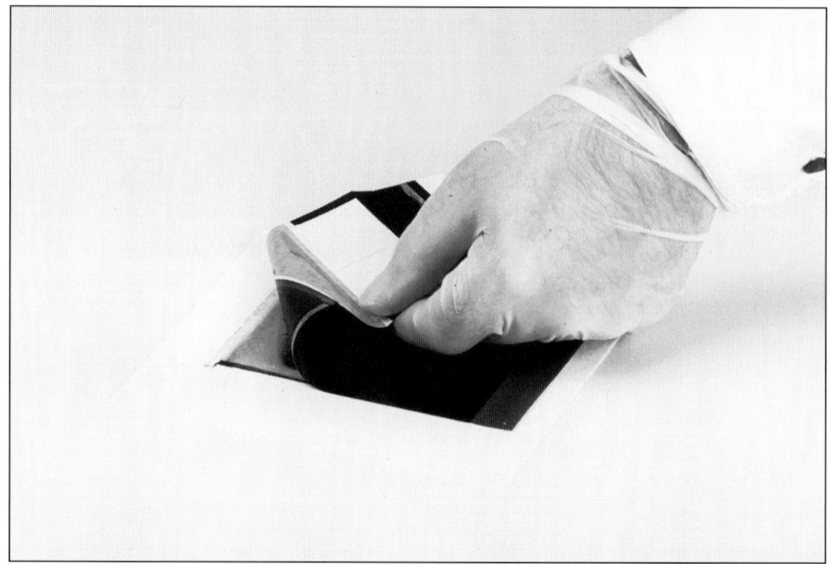

Fig. 3.18: *Lift tongue and bend back toward far corner. Break bond at corner.*

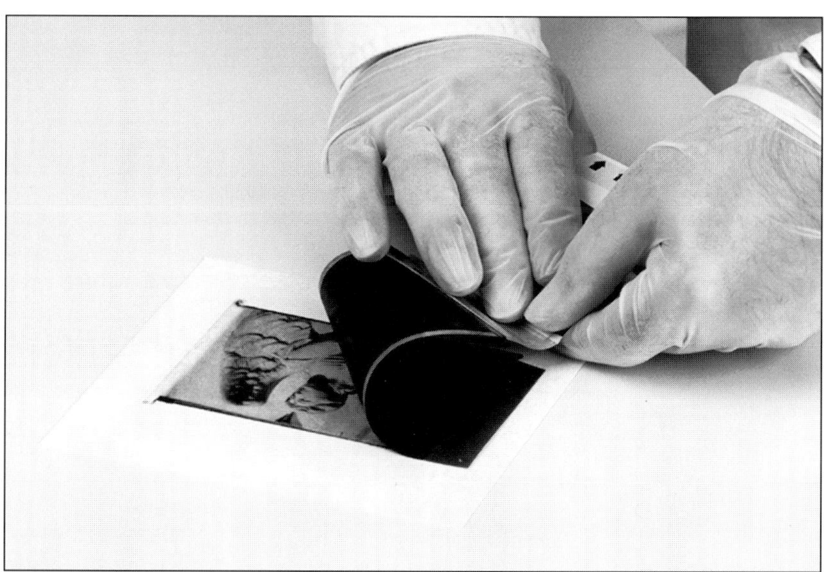

Fig. 3.19: *Pull off with an unhesitating motion and discard.*

released from the receptor, then discard it *(fig. 3.19).* Polaroid carriers are good for only one shot.

There's your first Polaroid transfer, and good or bad, there's nothing like seeing the first one revealed.

Remove Excess Chemistry. Because the development pod always leaves chemicals behind, which dry as a brown stain, you may wish to clean off some of the remaining chemistry from that edge of the image. Use a damp paper towel and a rolling wrist motion to absorb the reagent. You could also hold the watercolor paper image-side-up directly under a slow running cool tap and rub the chemistry off with a fingertip (wear a glove). Avoid rubbing the image area itself, and do not get the image area any more wet than absolutely necessary – and then only on the very edge.

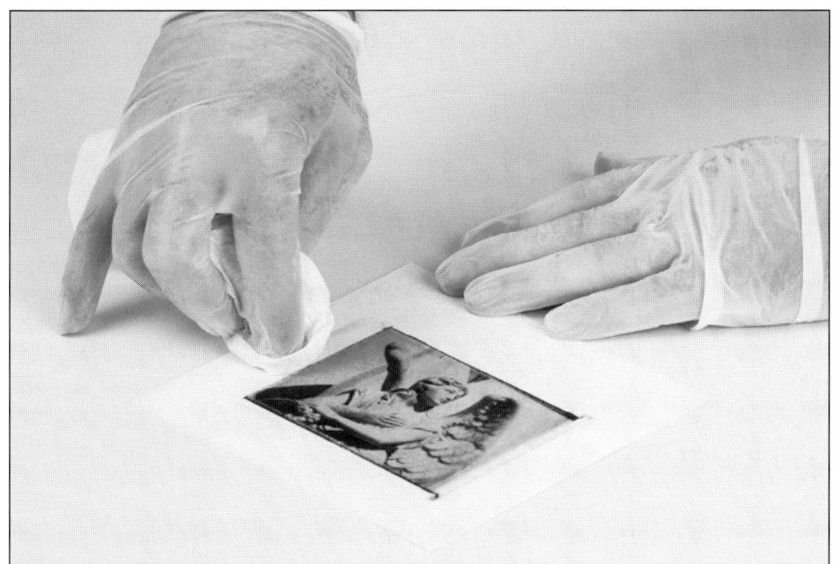

Fig. 3.20: *Use a wet paper towel to remove the leftover reagent at the "bottom" of the image. Set transfer aside to dry.*

Wet emulsion can bubble up where excessively wet and those bubbles may break, leaving small circles of clean paper.

Drying. After removing the excess chemistry, lay the transfer on a clean, dry, waterproof surface to dry flat, or hang it from a clean clothesline with spring type clothes pins.

After the print is dry, use a dry mount press or household iron to flatten the print. Low heat (180°F or 82°C) is perfect. Place a clean, dry towel or sheet of white, unlined paper between the iron and the transfer before pressing.

There is always some density shift between wet and dry transfers (all dry darker than when wet – it's called "drydown"), so don't render final judgment of your image until it's dry and flat. Keeping a log of exposure, imbibe time, filtration, etc., is a good idea in order to make corrections at a later time.

Chapter 4

SPECIAL IMAGE TRANSFER TECHNIQUES

• ALTERNATE TRANSFER PROCEDURE #1

Many photographers feel their transfer results are better if heat is used somewhere along the line. Like manipulating effects through imbibe time differences, you may find the careful application of heat at one stage or another will affect your work by influencing color or texture or in another way that contributes to your personal "look."

Heated Receptor. For this first alternative you can use any wet receptor you wish, although we will assume you are using a consistent-result producing paper, such as Arches. This procedure is simple: thoroughly soak the receptor in hot water until you need it, then remove, drain a bit and place the carrier on the work surface prior to beginning the transfer process. You will need a source for hot water – a stable temperature of 105°F (55°C) works well and is not too hot to handle *(fig. 4.1)*. You may find a higher temperature produces results more to your liking. (Always use a thermometer to verify temperature before sticking your hand, finger or any other appendage into hot water.)

There are two ways to approach this heat dependent method. The obvious first is to soak the receptors in the hot water until ready for transfer, at which time you will remove one receptor piece, drain slightly and place the carrier upon it, then begin the rub. Timing is somewhat critical, as you do not want the receptor sheet to cool before contact with the carrier. Using a thirty second imbibe time, you can make the exposure and begin the development process before pulling the hot receptor sheet from the water bath. After beginning development, pull a receptor sheet, drain slightly before placing it onto the transfer surface and

QUICK TIPS:

The best and most affordable heater I've found is a used electric skillet, available at garage sales and second hand stores for next to nothing, or new, for a higher price, of course, at discount/department stores.

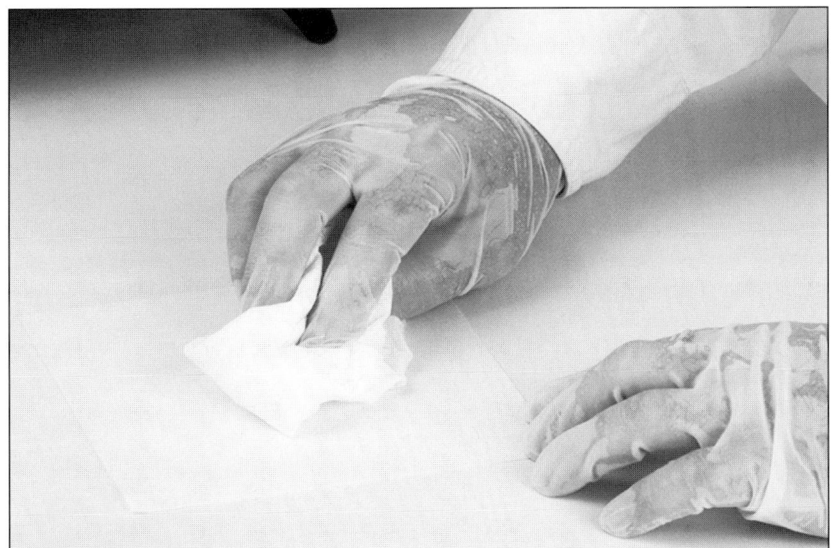

Fig. 4.1: *With hot water ready, prepare paper as before.*

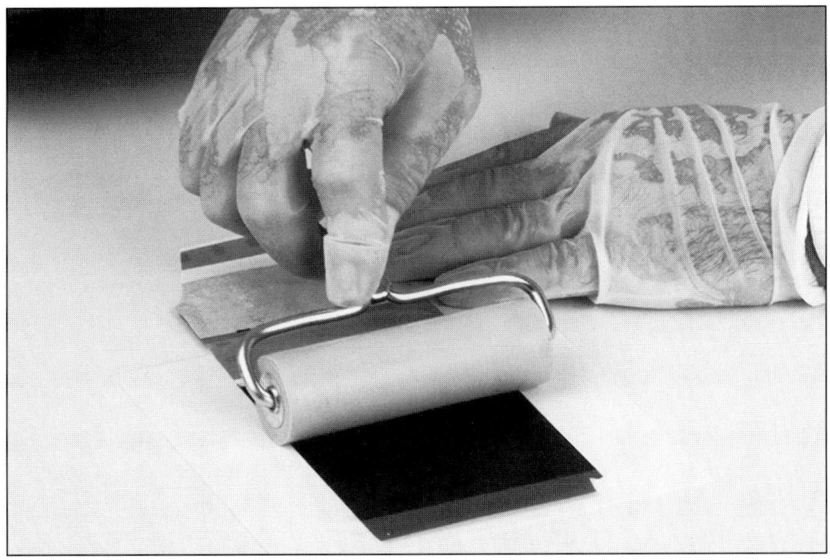

Fig. 4.2: *After the exposed film has been laid down, roll in both directions for two minutes.*

then soak up about 50% of the remaining water with paper towels. It will still be warmer than room temperature when you contact the carrier to it. Make contact and rub for two minutes *(fig. 4.2)*.

If you want to keep your work surface warmer, and thus maintain the temperature of the receptor longer, use a microwave oven to heat a damp, folded bath towel to steaming hot. *Never handle the steaming towel with bare hands.* Use tongs or a similar device to remove the very hot towel and place it on the work surface for several minutes. Immediately prior to placing the receptor sheet, use the tongs again to move the towel safely out of your way. Your receptor will stay hotter much longer and will transfer some of its heat all the way up to the carrier sheet. Be careful. Steam burns are nasty and painful.

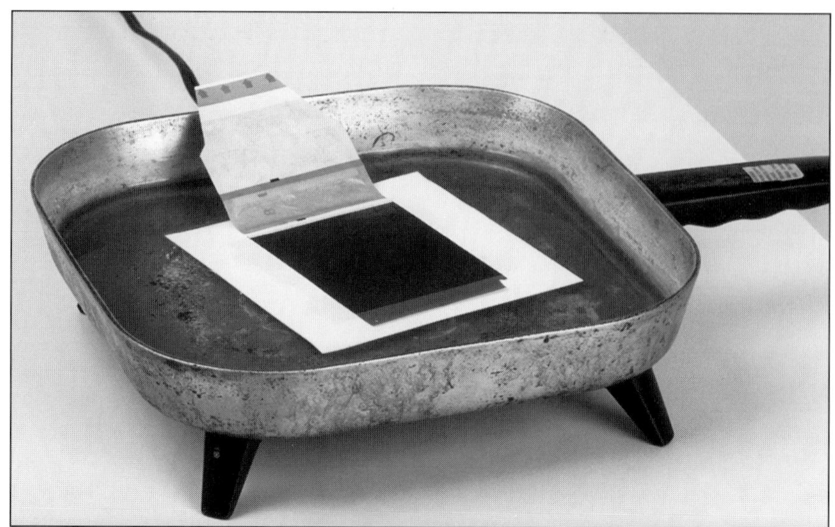

Fig. 4.3: *Float both pieces on the hot water surface for two to five minutes.*

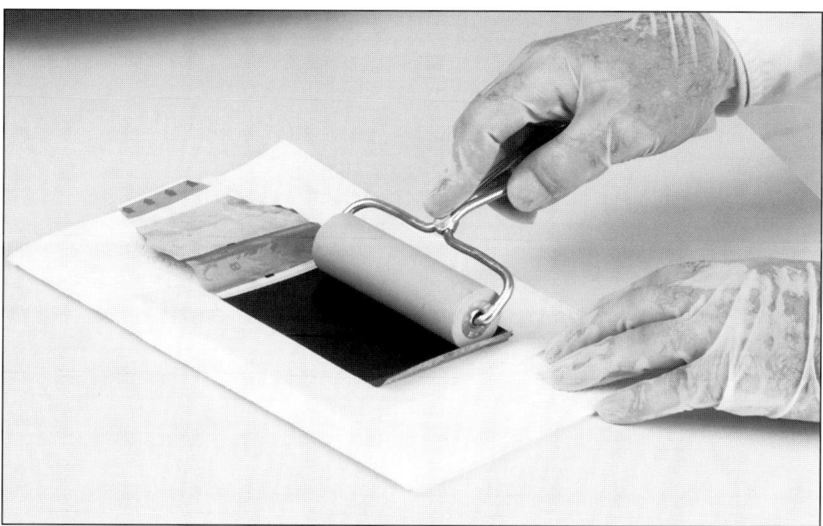

Fig. 4.4: *Roll over entire paper surface to blot excess water.*

Heated Carrier and Receptor. The second approach takes a little more time but may be a bit easier. After beginning a transfer and rolling the carrier to the receptor for at least two minutes, float the receptor with the carrier still attached on top of the hot water for an additional two to five minutes *(fig. 4.3)*. Be careful to not sink the receptor below the waterline, which will flood and loosen the edges, if not the entire carrier sheet. This method allows the chemistry to cook with heat, accelerating the chemical bond without drying out the receptor.

Remove with a spatula when ready and place on a double layer of paper towels. Briefly roll in both directions beyond the edges of the carrier paper to absorb water accumulated during the extra soak *(fig. 4.4)*.

• ALTERNATE TRANSFER PROCEDURE #2

With this method, heat is applied to a room temperature receptor with a hair dryer after the negative has been placed. Immediately after contacting the two materials, and as you begin to press with your roller, turn on a portable hair dryer and aim the nozzle at the back of the Polaroid material from a distance of three to four inches. To avoid burns, keep your fingers out of the way. Use the nozzle to precede the roller so that you are always rolling over a hot surface *(fig. 4.5)*.

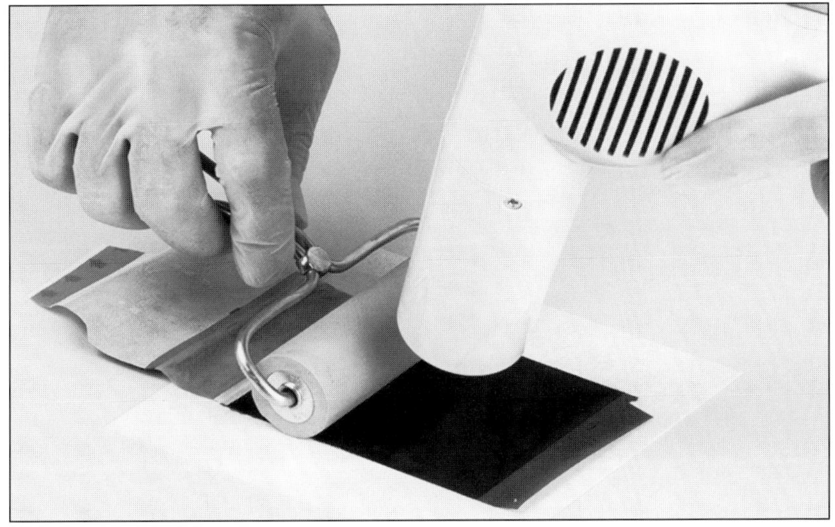

Fig. 4.5: *Precede the brayer with the hot air dryer for the entire two minute roll. All other steps are the same.*

You may notice a color shift toward the red. In color theory, red is an "advancing" color, meaning that a viewer will see it before any other colors that may be in the same image, sign or whatever. Thus, any overt red shift will be more visually prominent than a shift toward yellow or cyan. In fact, the red shift produced by heat-dependent procedures is usually enough to negate the slight cyan shift that normally accompanies a Type 108, 669, 59 or 809 transfer.

• ALTERNATE TRANSFER PROCEDURE #3

Short Imbibe Time. Many transfer artists like the rough texture and dark color that comes from a short imbibe time. At ten seconds, the dyes mix just enough to transfer minimal color. At thirty seconds, the dyes mix thoroughly and a finished Polaroid print requires only the additional build of contrast to be successful. As I said earlier, the thirty second imbibe time is the one I use the most, as I usually prefer the most detail and truest colors.

Even though a thirty second imbibe time and two minute roll is enough to achieve a successful image transfer, it's possible to get a smoother and more finely detailed transfer by continuing to roll beyond the minimum two minutes. For most of us, however, having to roll each image for many minutes more would cause high levels of boredom and serious loss of patience.

A transfer time of thirty *minutes* is desirable because the amount of transferred detail is maximized and may be achieved without rolling beyond the first two minutes. Place the wet transfer paper onto the work surface and remove the excess water, then coat the paper with Lysol® disinfectant spray *(fig. 4.5)*. Let it sit for at least fifteen seconds to penetrate, then wipe the excess from the surface. Be careful to not wipe too much; you must leave the paper wet enough to sustain a thirty minute contact (but not so wet that liquid oozes freely from the sides when rolling).

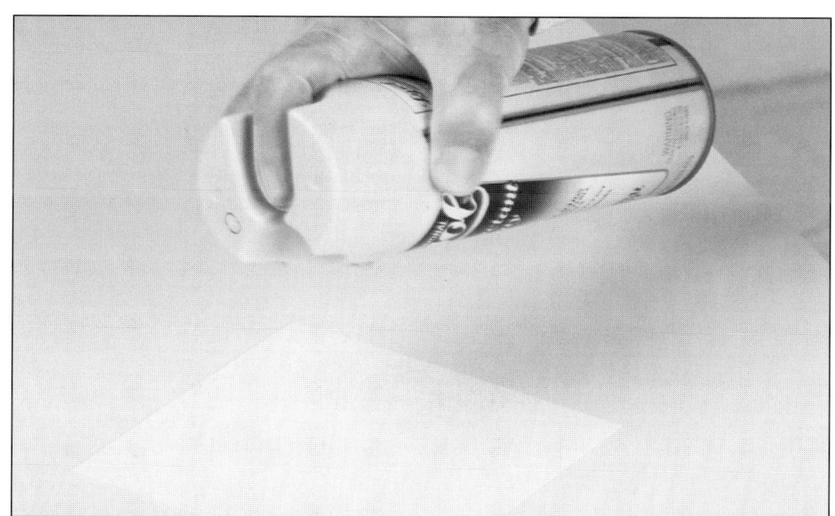

Fig. 4.6: *All prep steps are the same as basic steps, except the Lysol is sprayed on the paper after exposure and blotted before the carrier is placed. Roll for two minutes.*

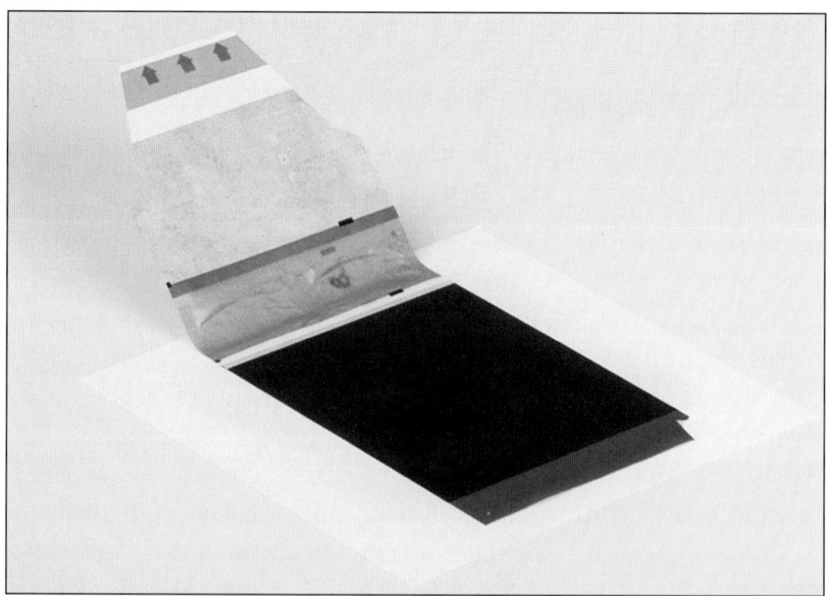

Fig. 4.6: *Print may be left for thirty minutes or longer to maximize transfer of color and saturation.*

Every other step is the same. Make the exposure, imbibe it, separate and lay the negative on the receptor. Roll the dyes into the receptor for two minutes, then walk away and let it sit. Peel your image apart thirty minutes or so later *(fig. 4.6)*. The difference is subtle but nonetheless amazing. Print texture is much smoother because the paper fibers have relaxed while maintaining contact with the carrier, and the dyes have transferred as much information as possible, resulting in a rich, detailed image.

"The difference is subtle but nonetheless amazing."

Transfers made with this technique are smoothest when using the soft rubber roller.

I believe this works as it does because the Polaroid chemistry is alkaline, as is the Lysol, which changes the pH of the neutral paper to something friendlier to Polaroid chemistry. I have had so much luck with this technique that I now use it automatically for almost every print I make. One word of caution – use only the "original scent" aerosol spray. The scented sprays have additional chemicals that sometimes leave a colored residue on your prints. You might also try mixing clear Lysol liquid into the soak bath, approximately two tablespoons per gallon.

• Contributors to Quality

There are a number of factors that contribute to the overall quality of any Polaroid transfer. Chief among the detractors is when the emulsion sticks to the receptor while you're trying to remove it.

Generally speaking, the areas of maximum density, or D-Max, where shadow detail is least evident (if at all) is where you'll have the most trouble separating the carrier from the receptor. Shortly after you begin making transfers you'll notice how certain areas of the image may not adhere to the receptor, leaving behind an area of blue/cyan stain where the image, and the emulsion, should be. This is just one of the idiosyncrasies of Polaroid transfers that you will have to learn to live with. Even using the Lysol method with wet transfers cannot stop all instances of D-Max lift-off although it will significantly increase the number of successful transfers.

When pulling the carrier from the receptor, keep a close watch on the D-Max areas. You can pull slowly and monitor the image as it releases, but don't stop or let the released film fall back upon the image, as even the slightest reattachment will leave a telltale line on the transfer. If you see any dark areas that do not release quickly, sever them with

Quick Tips:

Some transfer aficionados believe that emulsion batches close to or just after their expiration dates work better for transfers than newer, softer emulsions.

It is extremely difficult to find emulsions close to expiration for sale in camera stores, for the material, at least the professional variety, is usually purchased wisely and none remains beyond expiration. I have been able to try a few boxes of close-dated or recently expired film for transfers and so can say that I personally think it's a myth. If anything, the color is somewhat different – not quite as true. It's fine to use for transfers, just not a miracle.

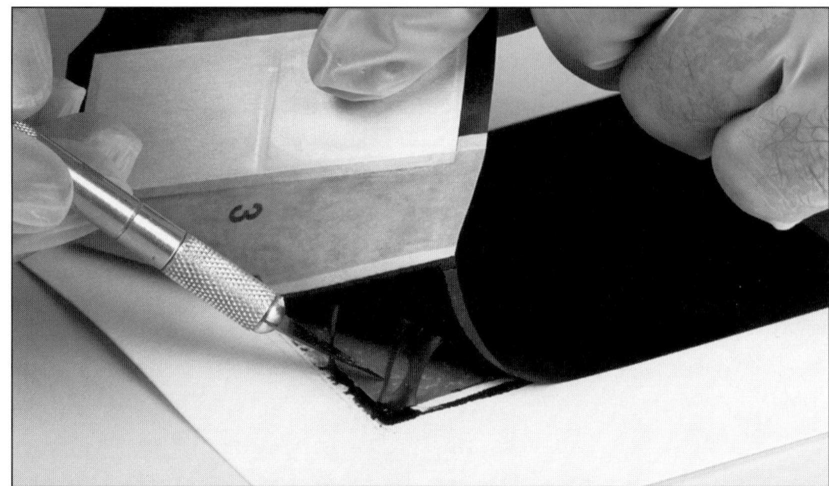

Fig. 4.7: *Use a graphic arts knife to cut dense areas that may not release between carrier and receptor.*

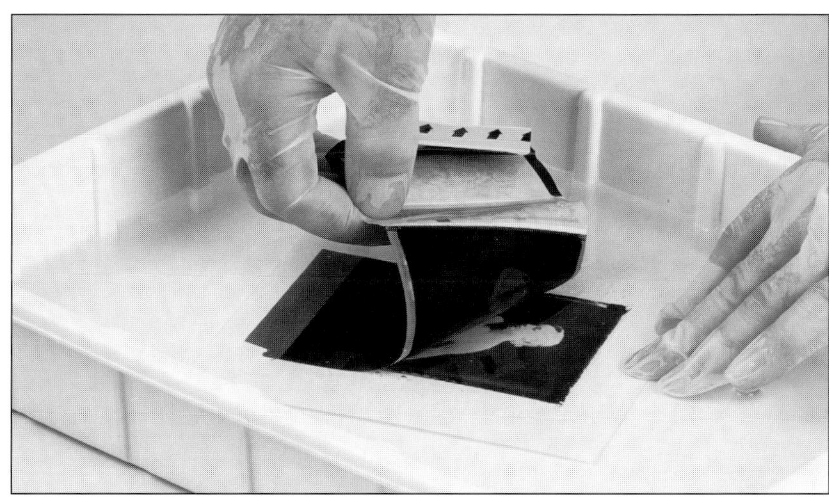

Fig. 4.8: *For images that will not print without sticking, separate under water.*

an X-Acto® or similar utility knife *(fig. 4.7)*. The severed emulsion that falls back onto the transfer image can be left as is or carefully moved around with the knife and pressed back into place after the carrier is completely removed.

If you have a continuing problem with emulsion adherence, you might try adding two ounces of Kodak Indicator Stop Bath to each gallon of soak water. You may also use household vinegar at one cup per gallon.

If all else fails and you cannot get the dark areas to release, try this. After completing the two minute roll, place the attached carrier and receptor in a separate tray of clean, room temperature water. Let them soak together for fifteen seconds. Keep both pieces underwater when peeling them apart – they should come apart easily – but remove immediately and drain thoroughly before setting to dry. If the paper is too wet, some bubbling may occur in the darker areas. You may also notice some staining that flows from the image in the direction of the drained water. It's dye from the partially dissolved emulsion.

Chapter 5

DRY TRANSFER TECHNIQUES

As the name implies, dry Polaroid transfer involves making a transfer to an unsoaked, dry receptor.

The materials needed for dry transfer are:

- Coated (glossy) paper or other paper of choice
- Rubber or nylon "J-Roller" or brayer
- Paper towels
- Disposable rubber surgical gloves
- Polaroid material of choice
- Correct equipment for printing method you have chosen

• MAKING THE FIRST DRY TRANSFER

Dry Receptors for Types 108, 669, 59 and 64T films. Paper, including watercolor paper like Arches, or other porous materials may be used without soaking, and sharp, colorful dry transfers may also be made on coated stock. Coated surfaces, called "enamel" in the paper business, must be hard enough so absorption is minimal (to retard the speed of moisture absorption) yet soft enough to allow the dyes to penetrate. Some of the best enamel surfaces I've found for dry transfers are Spectratech Gloss Coated Basis 70 (available from paper supply houses), and Canson Coated Airbrush paper (available from most graphic arts supply houses). Both papers give finely detailed, well saturated transfers but the Canson is thicker. If you can't maintain a good grip on the film or paper during the first few seconds of the transfer, you may see areas of broken or slipped dye. Like all variations of the Polaroid processes, you may be able to use this characteristic to your advantage.

"... colorful dry transfers may also be made on coated stock."

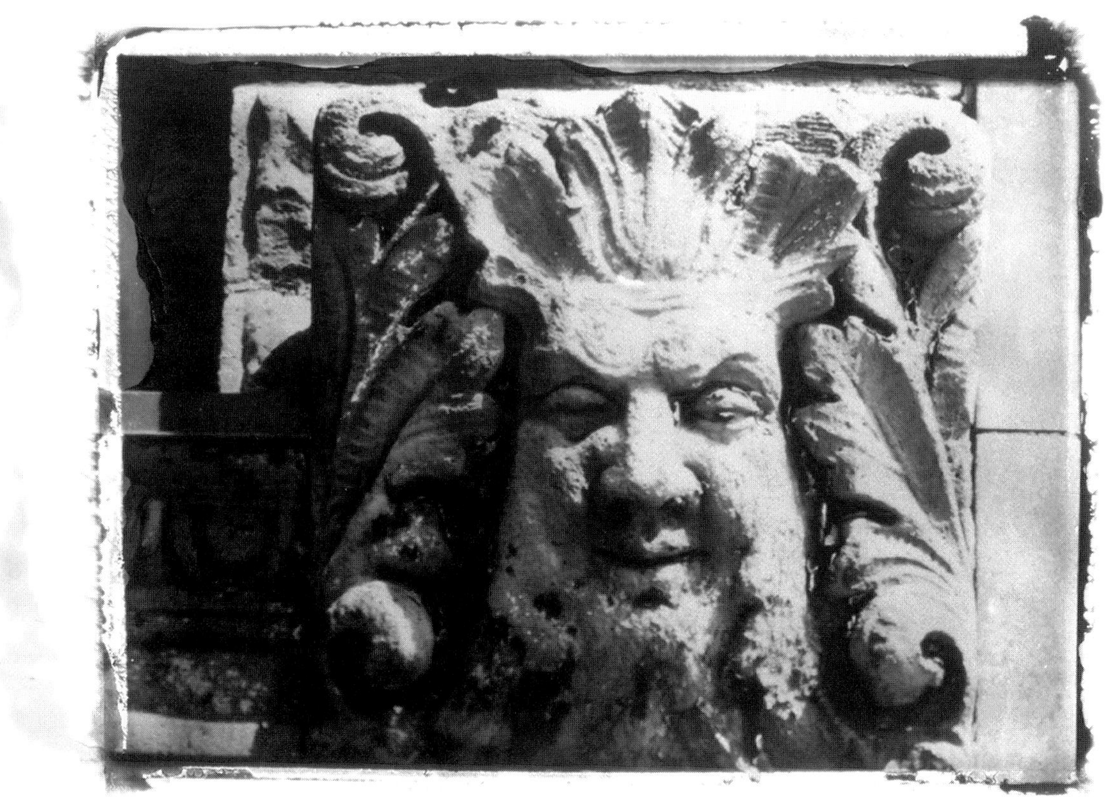

Fig. 5.1: *The experimental trial of dry transfer and Epson Ink Jet Paper (see text). Type 669.*

Surfaces like these work equally well with any transferable Polaroid stock.

Newsprint, vellum, parchment and many handmade papers may also be used. Each allows a different look to the finished product and each will require its own practice time. Papers such as Kromekote® or similar ultra shiny stocks (the enamel surface is too hard for the dye to penetrate), and artificial "papers" such as Kimdura® or Tyvek®, consistently produce what I feel are unsatisfactory results.

Recently, a moment of curiosity led me to find what I think is a superlative surface for dry transfers. Epson, a maker of fine inkjet printers, also sells packages of "Epson High Quality Ink Jet Paper" (#S041111), a non-glossy, text-weight sheet (about the thickness of this page) which works extremely well for dry transfers. I'll admit that the first time I tried it I didn't expect much. I merely made an exposure and rather absentmindedly rubbed it down for a perfunctory forty-five seconds. The result was spectacular – a dry transfer with smooth, even tones, and excellent color and saturation *(fig. 5.1)*.

The Dry Transfer Process. Follow the instructions given previously for exposure and imbibe time. Wear your gloves.

Have a piece of dry paper ready to go on a clean, flat surface. Lightweight dry papers should be tacked down across the corners with a removable artist tape *(fig. 5.2)*. Wet paper will bond itself to a flat surface, but dry paper tends to slide around. Dry paper will also buckle as moisture from the Polaroid dyes is absorbed. This may cause some broken image areas in the print or just make it difficult to roll evenly. A little practice with the material and paper is all it takes to find and work those bugs out.

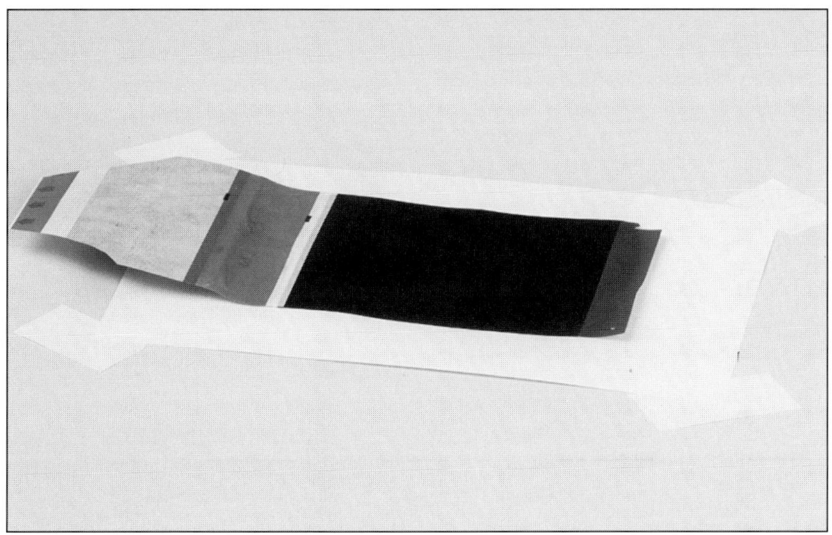

Fig. 5.2: *It may be necessary to tape the corners of thin paper when doing dry transfers.*

Practice will also tell you how long to leave the carrier on the paper you're using, but sixty seconds is probably the absolute maximum. Anything longer and the absorbed dyes begin to dry and the materials stick to each other, ripping both paper and Polaroid surfaces when pulled apart.

"Practice will also tell you how long to leave the carrier on the paper you're using ..."

After the transfer is pulled apart, you may wish to wipe off some of the leftover chemical reagent at the "bottom" of the image. With dry transfers, this residual goo dries a darker red-brown than it does with wet transfers, sometimes dark enough to distract from the image. Use a clean paper towel and wipe the goo off in one quick wrist-rolling motion. Don't press too hard – with a dry transfer it's easy to bring up some of the paper surface along with the reagent.

Remove any tape and move to a flat surface to complete drying. It won't take long, especially if you've wiped off the residual chemistry.

Flatten dry prints with an iron or dry mount press, using low heat (180°F or 82°C). Place a clean, unlined sheet of white paper between the iron (or press) and the print.

Chapter 6

TRANSFERS WITH POLACOLOR PRO 100 MATERIAL

"It will win you over if you give it a chance."

• WET TRANSFERS WITH POLACOLOR PRO 100 MATERIAL

Horror stories about how difficult it was to transfer this material began to circulate within days of its release. Most gripes centered around color troubles or adherence problems, but the longer processing time (ninety seconds at 70°-80°F (21°-27°C)) threw off imbibe time estimates, and many photographers had difficulty getting consistent results.

As a response to these concerns, Polaroid printed a set of guidelines based on its research. They recommend using hot water that has been treated with an acid such as household vinegar or a base such as baking soda, to change the pH of the soak bath, thus making watercolor paper more receptive to the new emulsion.

Maybe it's just the water in Minneapolis, but I can't say I've been forced to do anything special to achieve terrific results with PolaColor Pro 100. If anything is evident, it's that this material is sharper, richer in color and easier to clean up than the other color materials. It's eccentric sometimes, and perhaps intimidating because it's seen as hard to work with and not commonly referenced as a transfer medium. It will win you over if you give it a chance.

My first test used an image very rich in red and magenta, as I had expected the traditional cyan shift I'd seen with Type 669. I was very surprised to see almost no color shift at all, the transfer being quite true to the original. Done with my staple thirty second imbibe time, two minute rub with Lysol-sprayed paper technique (*fig. 6.1*), this first transfer was among the nicest, technically, that I'd ever created.

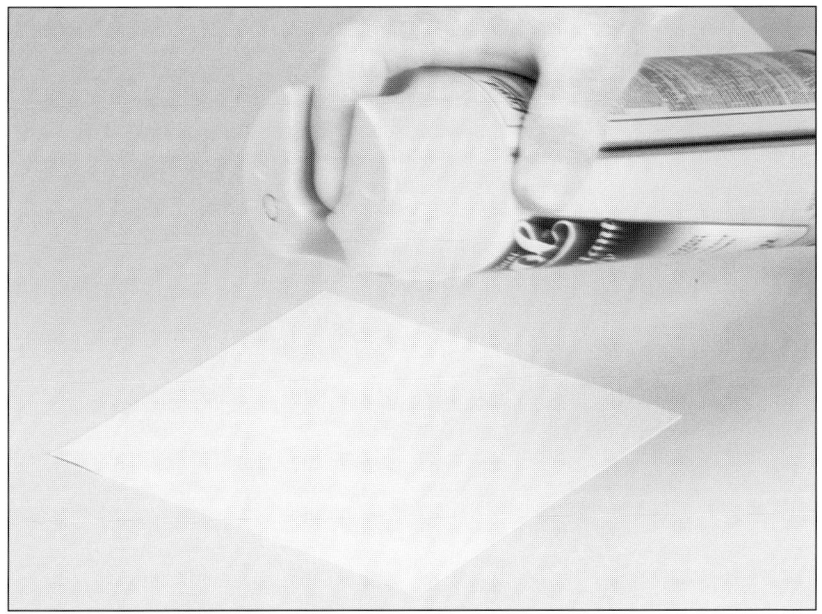

Fig. 6.1: *Use of Lysol spray is always recommended for Pro 100 transfers.*

I also tried a dry transfer onto Arches watercolor paper, pulling the carrier from the receptor after only one minute. With the soft rubber roller I was able to get an image so smooth and detailed it almost looked like a "real" photograph, yet it had character that set it in a class by itself.

Using Pro 100 appears to have other benefits as well. Because of the longer processing time, it seems to be more forgiving regarding imbibe time than its counterparts. A forty-five second imbibe time produces almost the same results as a thirty, so you may not need to scramble so fast. Also, the goo left at the bottom is practically invisible when dry, so you may not wish to clean that up, although your transfers will take longer to thoroughly dry. (Transfers flattened with heat show a very slight yellow cast in the residue area.) Finally, the dried borders are dark blue-black, not the usual cyan, and visually less intrusive.

After a few years of professional use, most of the bugs have been worked out and the emulsion is very consistent. In a finished transfer, the highlight areas may show a mottled, chartreuse color from leftover reagent chemistry. In many instances this merely adds visual interest, since it does not carry throughout the entire image. The overall amount of reagent color increases with increased imbibe time, however, and at some point you may want to clean some of it off. Do so with the area to be cleaned held under a slightly

QUICK TIPS:

Clean up the whites in your Pro 100 wet transfers by dipping them back into a soak bath for a few seconds (a separate tray), letting them drain slightly, and then running a squeegee over the image. Start at the end furthest from the chemical pod residue, as this wipes most of the sludge off the whites and takes the residual chemistry away at the same time. Proper pressure will be determined by practice. You may also go in with a cotton swab, to selectively clean whites in eyes and teeth, leaving other areas alone. The result is a dramatic difference in colors and, consequently, viewer perception of the subject is enhanced.

Fig. 6.2: *Remaining reagent on Pro 100 transfers may be removed by soaking under lightly running warm tap water and using a cotton swab. Type 679, Arches paper.*

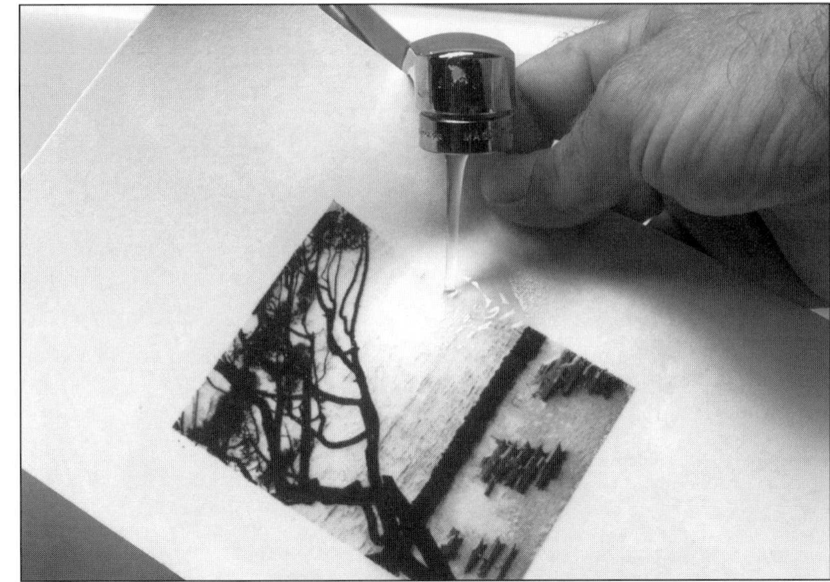

Fig. 6.3: *A long imbibe time allowed substantial amounts of reagent to build up on the surface of this print. Slightly overscrubbed, much was left to aid visual texture. Type 679, Arches paper.*

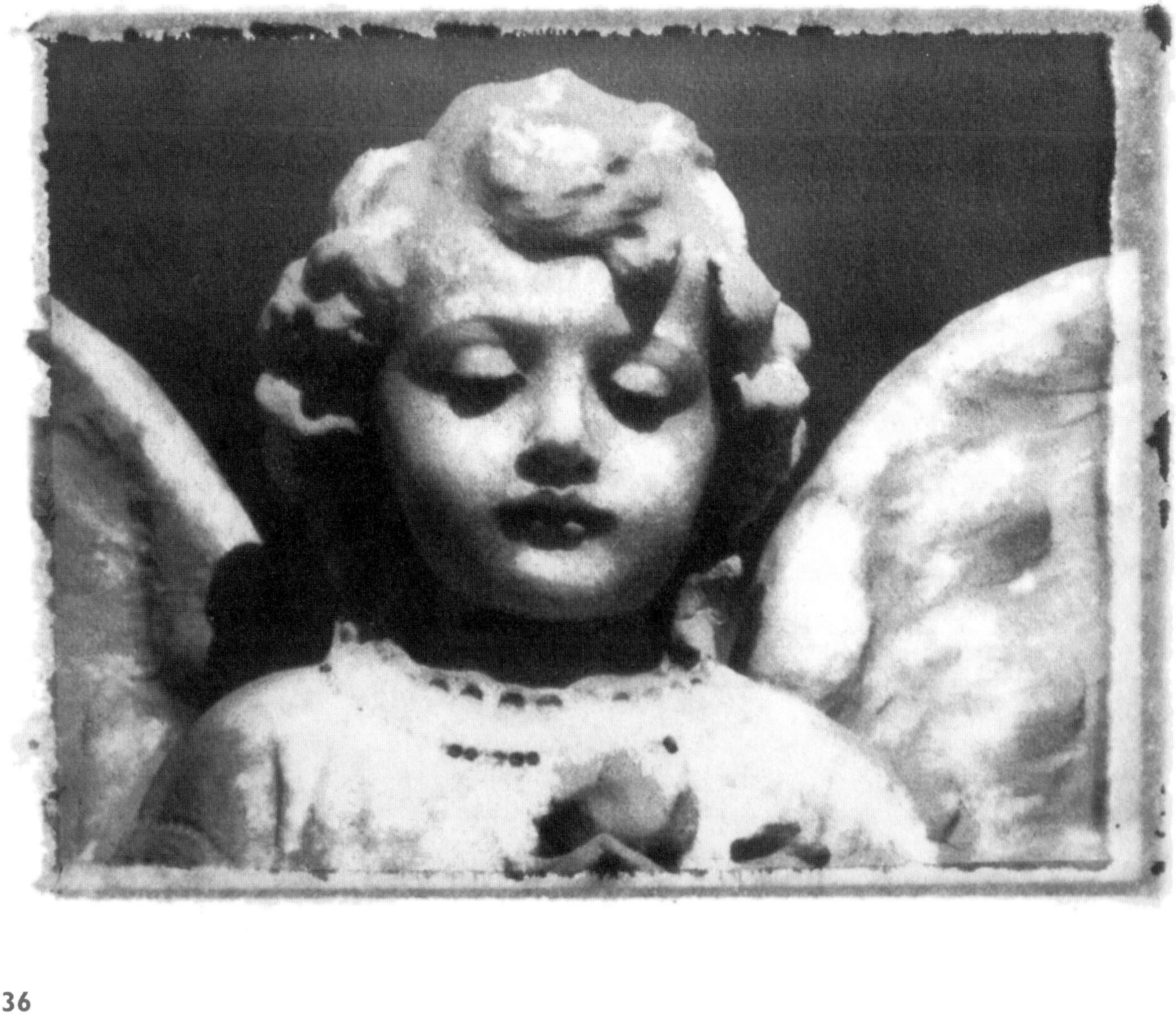

open water tap. Set the temperature at approximately 105°F (40°C) and run the water with almost no force at all. Let the paper soak under the hot water for a minute or so – don't let the water directly hit the image, just wash over it. After the emulsion has soaked under the hot water, use a cotton swab, and, with very light pressure, remove the reagent from the surface *(fig. 6.2)*. You run the risk of taking up the darker details of the image along with the reagent if you overdo it, but Pro 100 emulsions are more durable than others and will take more abuse.

With that in mind, you might want to deliberately remove more detail than is necessary. I call it "overscrubbing", and the results can be spectacular. By eliminating middle tones, apparent contrast is increased, sometimes achieving an almost "orthochromatic" look of pure black and white (or as close to it as Polaroid can get). When overscrubbing an image with large areas of median tones, do not scrub them evenly – apply pressure to eliminate some areas completely, others almost not at all *(fig. 6.3)*. Try combining overscrubbing with longer imbibe times – forty-five to sixty seconds – so as to increase the leftover reagent.

QUICK TIPS:

With Pro 100, the emulsion doesn't bubble when resoaked like it does with other material, so it will withstand rougher handling and deeper cleaning when wet. If you use a squeegee to remove water and chemistry, be aware of how much pressure you're applying – light pressure will remove some surface image and remaining reagent while heavier pressure will remove overall density from the image itself. Removing density creates a more pastel look to each color without changing the relationship of the colors to the image.

•ALTERNATE PRO 100 TRANSFER PROCEDURE #1 (THE HOT IRON PROCESS)

I didn't think it was possible to improve on the Pro 100 transfer process, but I may have found a way. Discovered while investigating the effects of heat on Pro 100 material, it is faster than any other technique, leaves minimal reagent on the image and seems to make the emulsion more durable for cleaning or other manipulation before drying *(fig. 6.4)*.

You will need a stable source of heat, about 200°F (93°C). I went to a thrift store where I found and purchased a "dry" (no steam vents) iron for $3.00. You don't need expensive or elegant tools for this process, only clean ones, a point made evident by my second-hand iron. You could use your household iron, but sooner or later you'll get chemistry on the platen, which Murphy's Law says you won't notice until you iron the collar on your favorite white shirt. If you use a steam iron, be certain the steam function is inoperative.

You should also buy a large sable hair brush. Camera store dust brushes work fine but are small and can be pricey. Makeup (blush) brushes are larger, moderately priced and hold more water within the hairs which makes them less abrasive to the print when the emulsion is being cleaned.

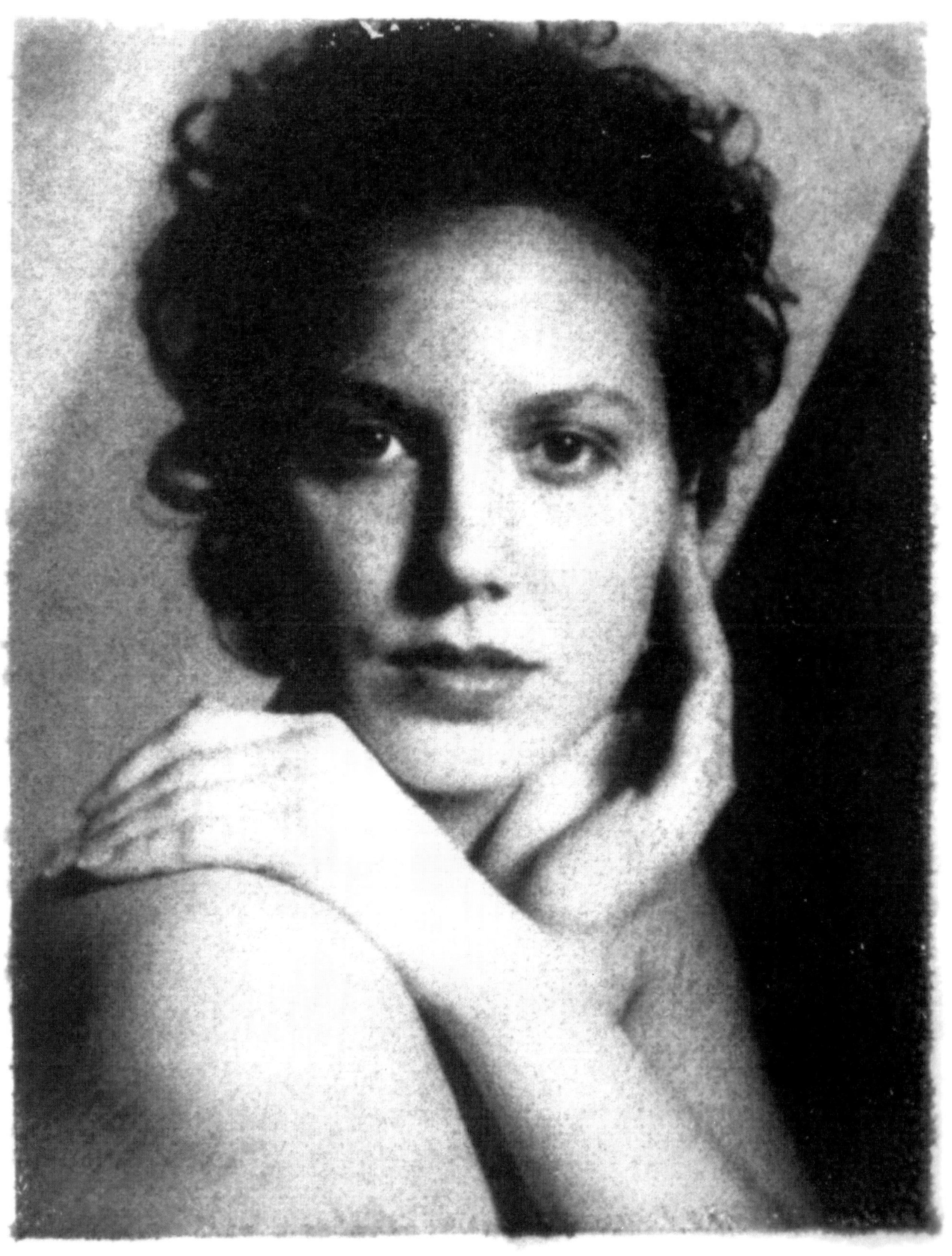

Fig. 6.4: *This Pro 100 image was cleaned and softened under running water without losing any fine detail. Type 679, Arches paper.*

For a wet transfer, soak the paper as usual in clean water. Drain when ready and wipe about 75% of the remaining liquid *(fig. 6.5)*, then either lift the paper and wipe under it or place the paper on a dry section of worktable. Finally, spray a heavy coat of Lysol *(fig. 6.6)* over the entire sheet. Make the exposure and imbibe for thirty seconds. At about twenty-five seconds *(fig. 6.7)*, flip the receptor paper onto the wet side *(fig. 6.8)*, then peel the Polaroid material and place the carrier on the receptor. Using the soft rubber roller, roll just enough to anchor the material *(fig. 6.9)*, two to three seconds. Place a clean sheet of plain white paper over the transfer *(fig. 6.10)* and apply the hot iron, rubbing in a circular motion (don't dawdle or let the iron rest) and with moderate pressure for at least five seconds but no more than ten *(fig. 6.11)*. Peel the image apart right away *(fig. 6.12)*.

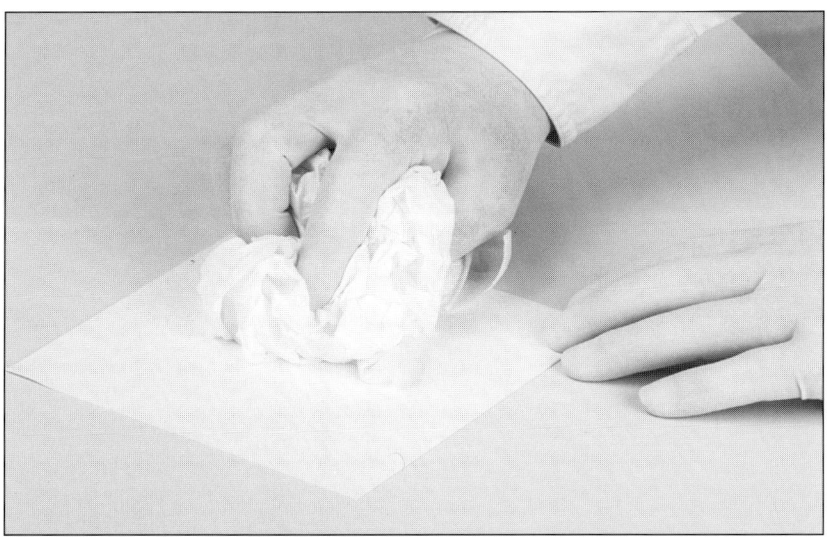

Fig. 6.5: *Wipe and absorb approximately 75% of water.*

Fig. 6.6: *Spray heavy coat of Lysol (surface should show puddles) and let it soak.*

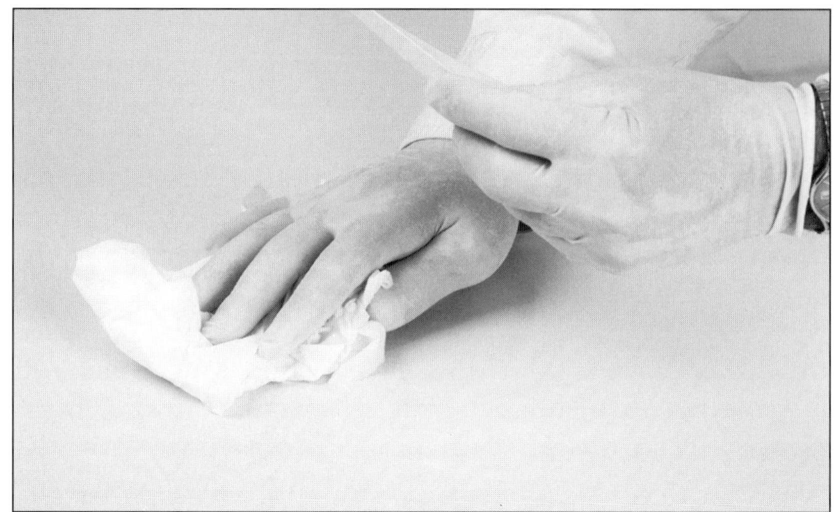

Fig. 6.7: *Prior to placing the carrier, lift receptor and wipe underneath.*

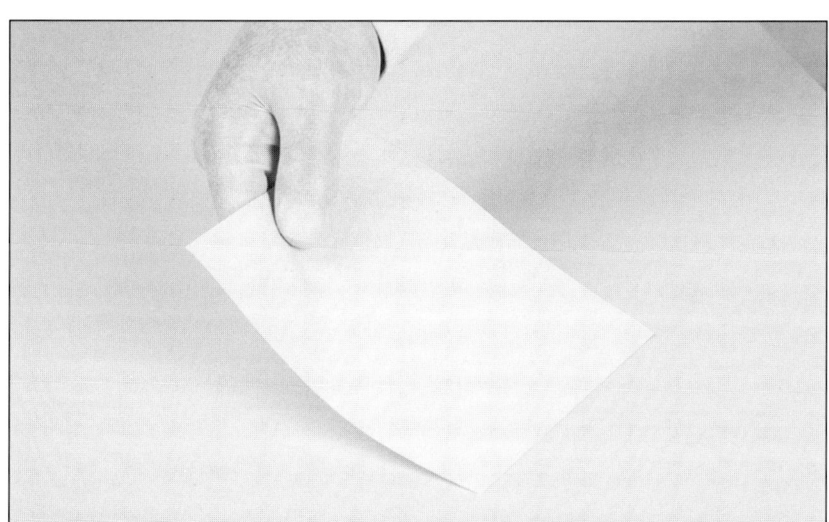

Fig. 6.8: *Flip receptor sheet over and place on work surface.*

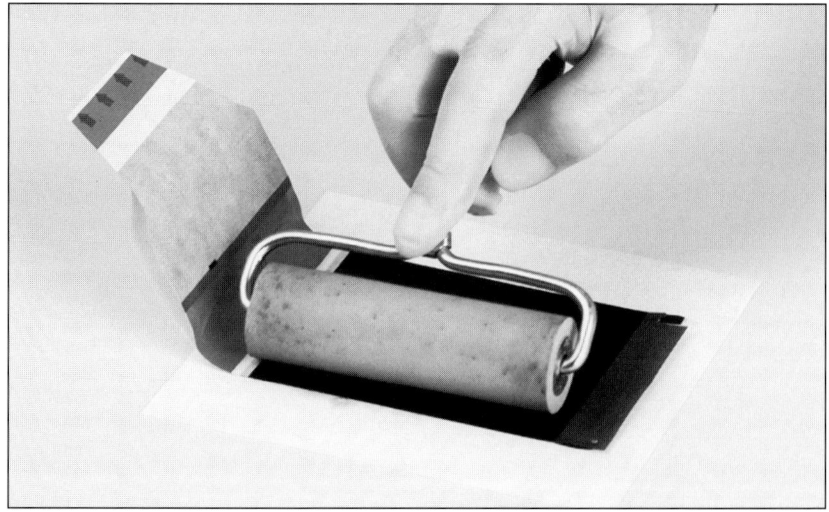

Fig. 6.9: *Two or three strokes in each direction is all that's necessary to anchor the carrier.*

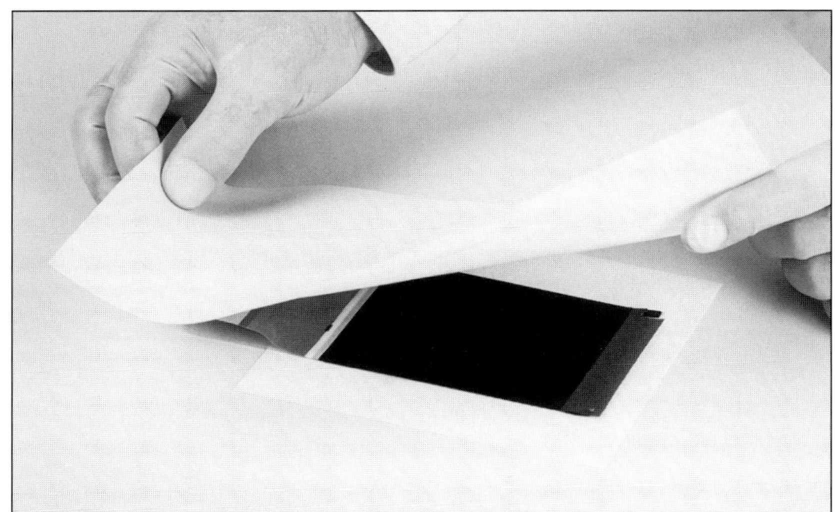

Fig. 6.10: *Place clean sheet of white paper over carrier and receptor.*

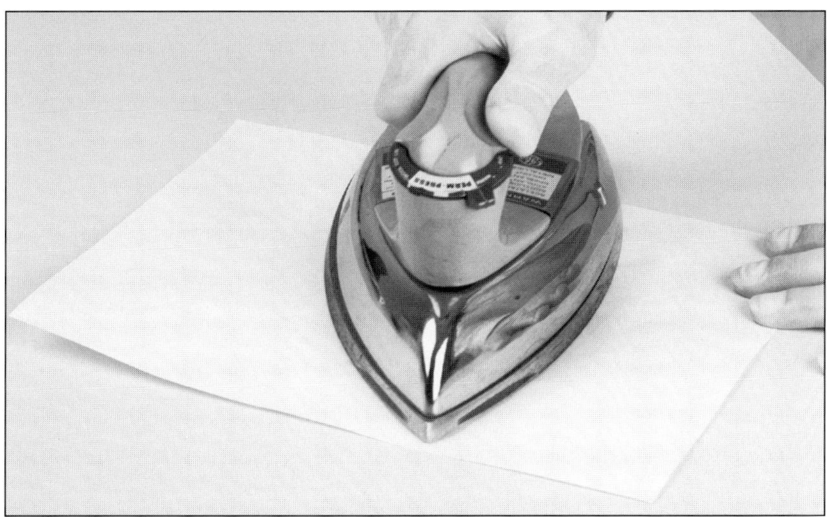

Fig. 6.11: *With immediate circular and moderate pressure, press with hot iron for five to ten seconds.*

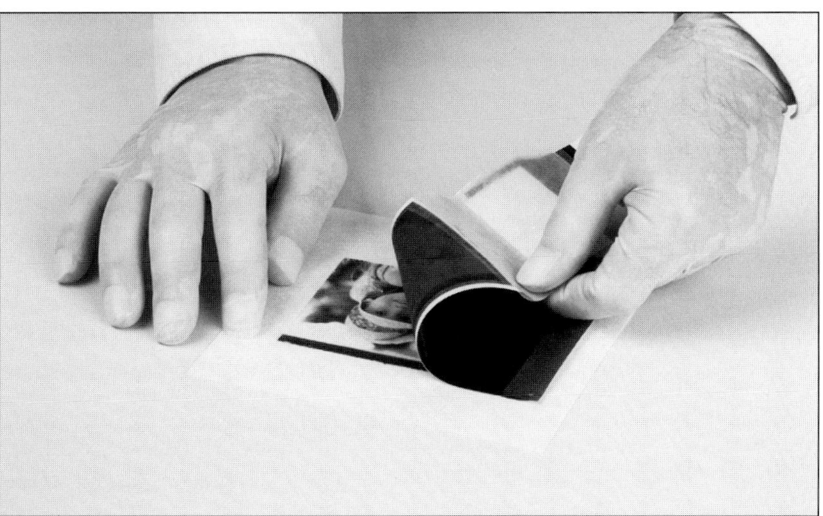

Fig. 6.12: *Break seal and peel immediately.*

This new transfer should surprise you with its depth and clarity. Sharper than any other wet transfer, it also shows more shadow detail.

To remove minor traces of reagent remaining on the surface, either submerge the print for a short time in warm (105°F or 40°C) water or get it wet under a slightly running tap. Thoroughly soak the brush in the same water and hold the brush handle parallel to the surface of the picture. Let the weight of the water bend the bristles down to the paper and *very lightly* glide the bristles over the surface, just barely touching the emulsion *(fig. 6.13)*. This minimal pressure will also clean up most minor inconsistencies found in areas of even tone, resulting in a superior, creamy smooth picture.

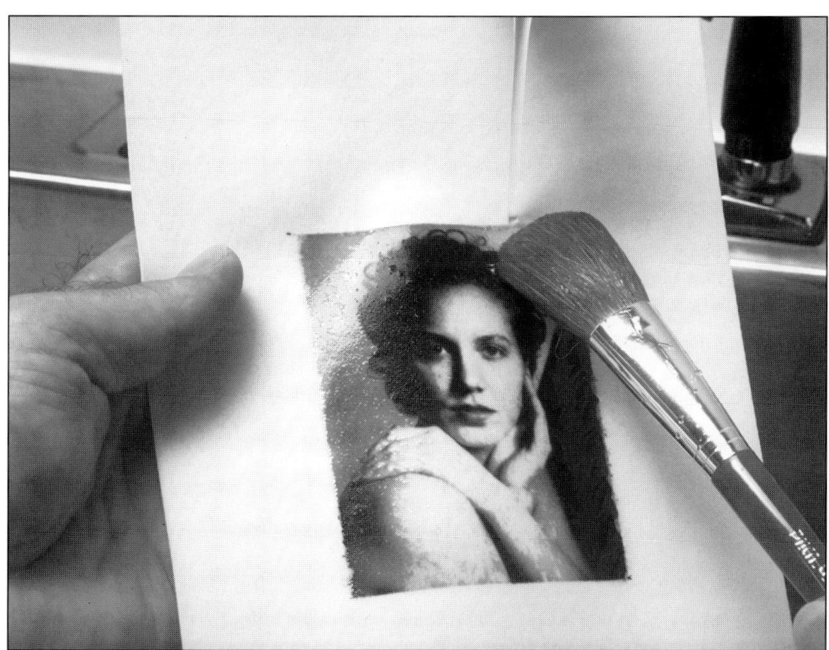

Fig. 6.13: *Pro 100 transfers may be cleaned overall by soaking under lightly running warm tap water and using a large, wet, soft-bristled brush.*

• DRY TRANSFER WITH PRO 100 MATERIAL

As with other Polaroid materials, Pro 100 dry transfers can be made onto any of the surfaces listed above. Imbibe times of thirty to forty-five seconds seem to work best, followed by a sixty second maximum contact between carrier and receptor. As with wet transfers, remaining reagent may be cleaned off with a wet cotton swab.

Polaroid Corporation also markets a glossy paper, intended for use with inkjet printers, that produces very interesting results when used as a dry receptor for Pro 100 transfers. Since this is not a fiber base paper, it is very water-resistant and will not absorb much moisture from the Polaroid negative. One should not place the paper under running water or soak it in a tray after transfer, as the emulsion, in an attempt to expand as it gets wet (yet firmly anchored to the paper), acquires a crinkled texture reminiscent of stained glass.

After removing the carrier sheet, any remaining reagent can be cleaned with a wet cotton swab. When finished, blot any excess water by pressing lightly with a paper towel. Any blotting over the image itself should be done by laying a loose sheet of paper towel onto the image area and soaking up water without pressing the paper.

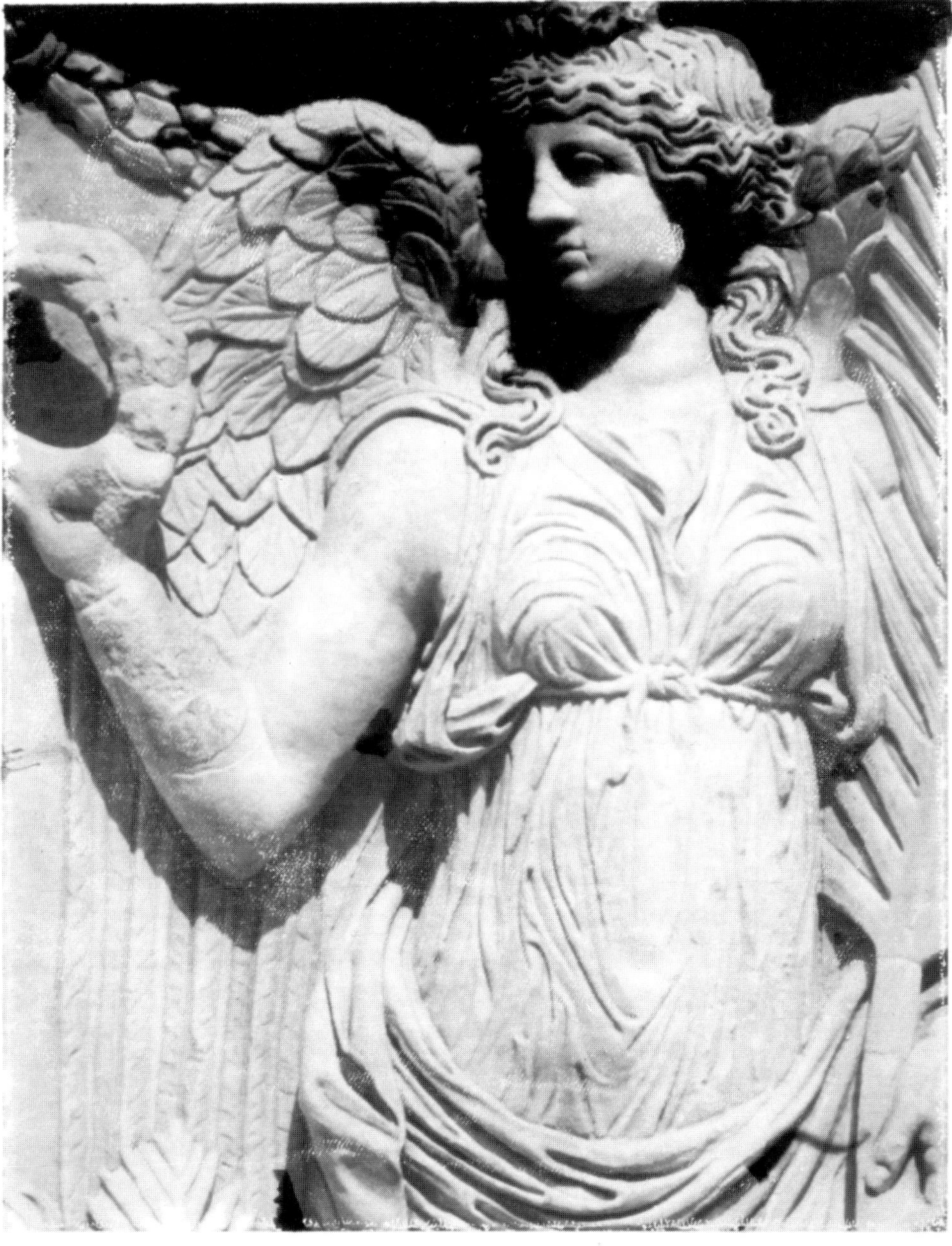

Fig. 6.14: *Depending upon the image, Polaroid, and other inkjet papers, may produce almost true photographic results.*

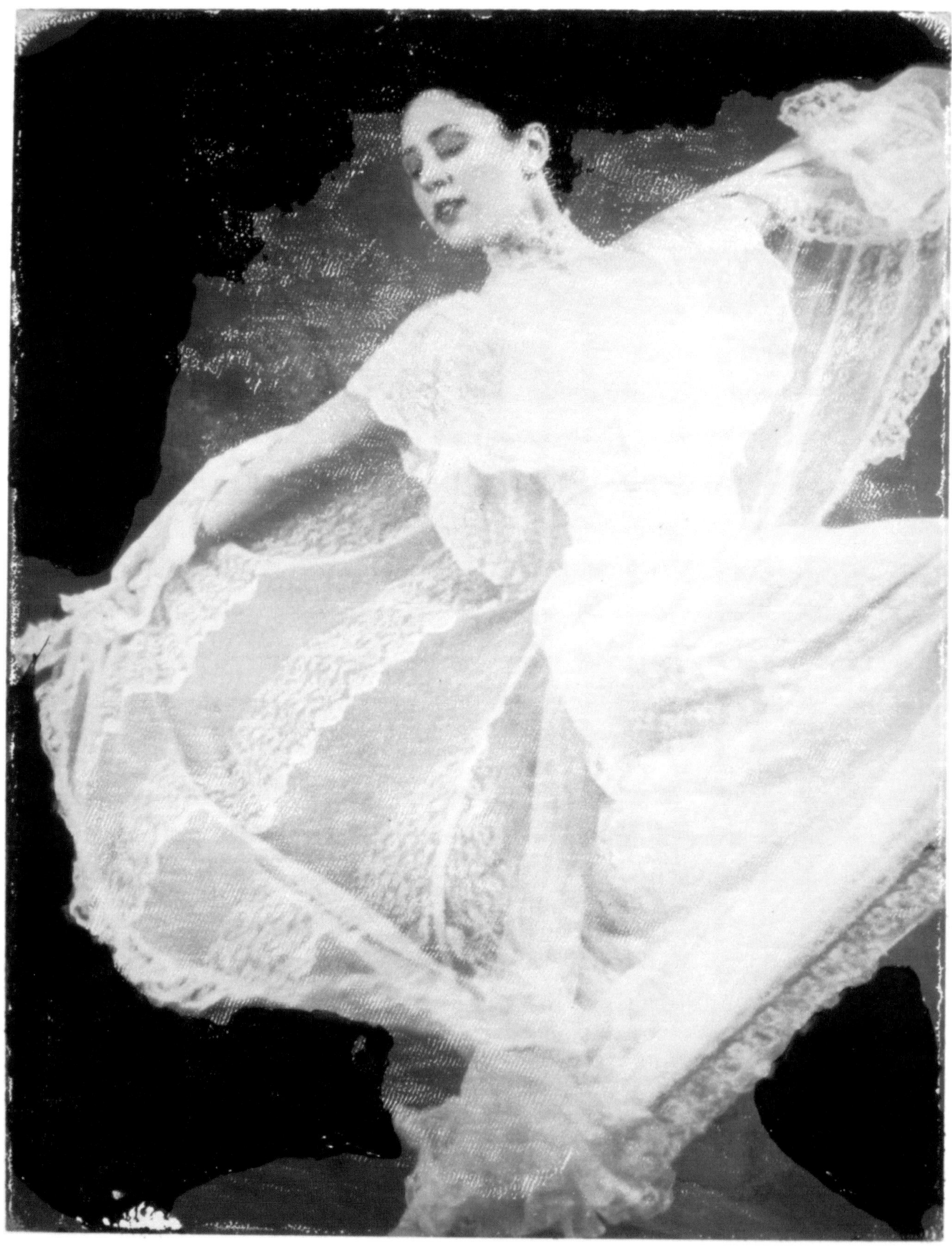

Fig. 6.15: *Extremely interesting effects can be accomplished by dry transferring Polaroid to inkjet printing papers such as those made by Polaroid.*

Chapter 7

TIPS AND TRICKS FOR IMAGE TRANSFER

• IMBIBE TIMES AND EXPOSURE

Here's a way to get an accurate understanding of how imbibe times and exposures affect Polaroid transfers. This is most easily accomplished with the Vivitar or Polaroid printer, but it will work with any method. If you are projection printing in the darkroom, be certain you find the correct exposure for a normal print before you begin this test. "Correct" exposure is that which looks as much like the original image as is possible. Using a slide that is well exposed, with good color and a wide range of tone, make a correct, normal exposure. Process the print for the full recommended time depending on ambient temperature. Let the final print dry thoroughly to most accurately judge color and density.

"... these will effectively indicate what exposure variations will do to your transfers."

With enough wet or dry material handy, make a series of eight exposures, all exactly the same, one at a time. With the first, let it imbibe ten seconds before separating and laying it down. Roll the brayer across it for two minutes, peel it apart and set it aside. Imbibe the next for fifteen seconds, then twenty, twenty-five, thirty, thirty-five, forty and forty-five seconds, respectively. When dry, it will be easy to see a correlation between imbibe time, texture and color transfer. Choose whichever you like the most. Make this your benchmark for imbibe times. You may wish to refer to the series of images on pages 17-19 for an example of such a series.

Using your benchmark imbibe time, make another series of exposures at -1, -1/2, +1/2, and +1 stop. When dry, these will effectively indicate what exposure variations will do to your transfers.

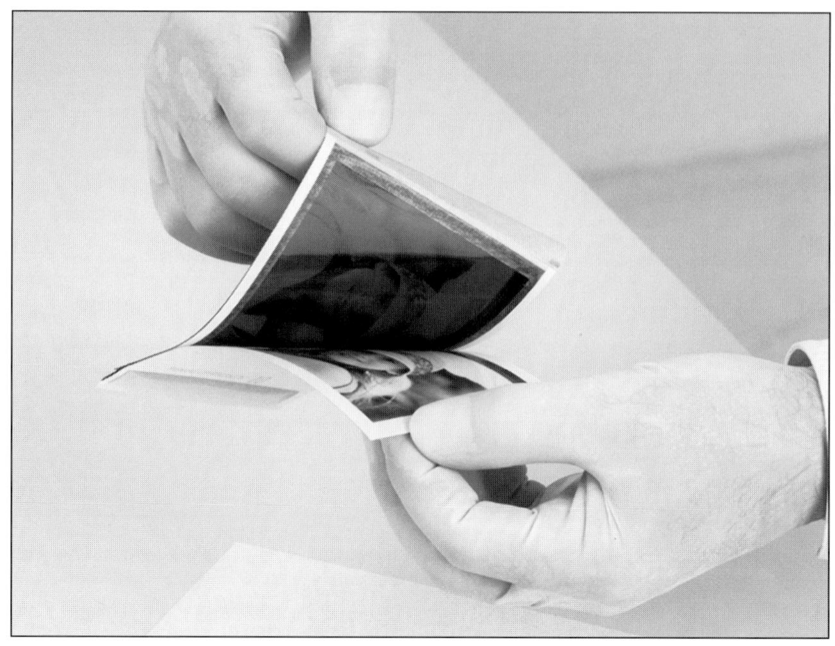

Fig. 7.1: *For even borders with Pro 100 transfers, peel the positive directly from the carrier, leaving the wax paper borders in place. Discard positive.*

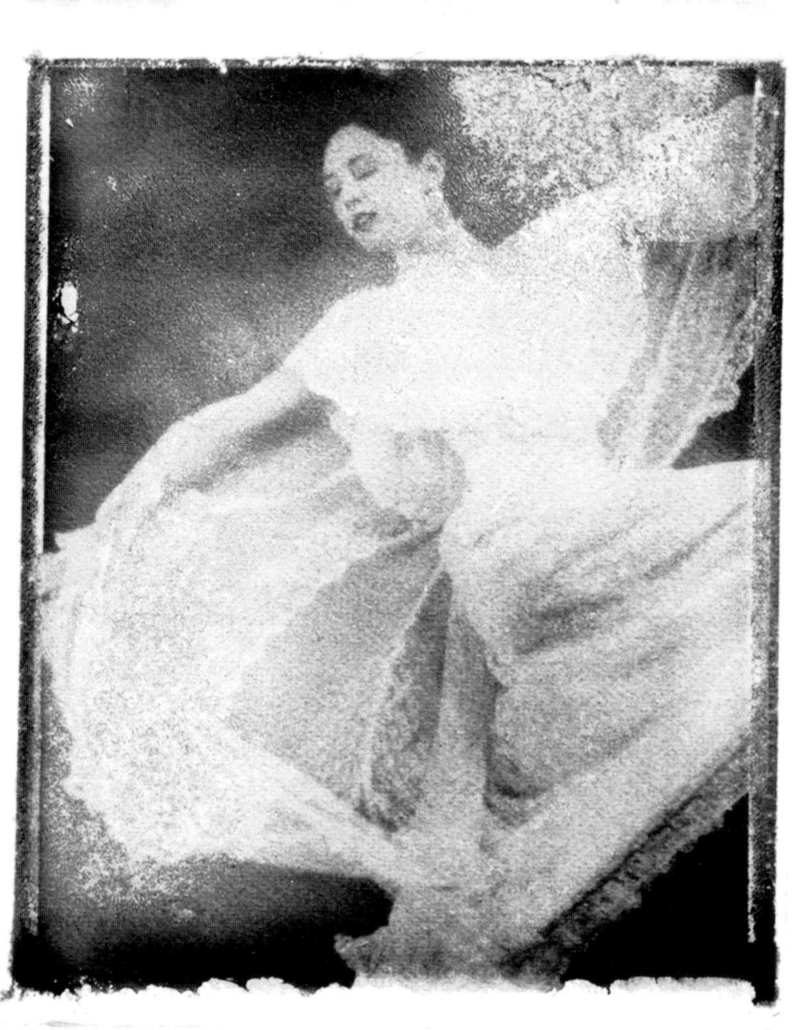

Fig. 7.2: *Cooking Polaroid film in a microwave for a few seconds during development may produce beautiful variations, but will not be repeatable.*

• Borderless Prints

If you would like transfers without the chemical borders that characterize them, peel the print straight off the carrier sheet, keeping the chemistry under the Polaroid border paper *(fig. 7.1)*. This works best with Pro 100 materials.

• Quick Dry

Wet transfers can be quickly dried in a microwave oven. Place the wet paper on a paper plate. At half power, cook it for two minutes. You may have to adjust final drying time to your own equipment.

• Microwave for Effect

Speaking of microwaves, you can also achieve some very interesting effects by zapping the exposed film. Immediately after the exposure has been pulled, and imbibe time started, cut off any metal tabs or clips on the Polaroid material. Place in microwave and, under high power, zap for two or three *seconds*. Peel at the end of the completed imbibe time and transfer normally. Results can be quite interesting, but will never be repeatable *(fig. 7.2)*.

"... you can also achieve some very interesting effects by zapping the exposed film."

• Over/Under Exposure

Underexposed originals will always transfer better than overexposed because exposure can be increased as much as necessary to optimize an image. Generally speaking, overexposed originals do not transfer well, since highlight tones will be blown out and show little more than the underlying paper surface. There is nothing you can do to fix that loss of detail, although you may try printing it -1 stop (or more) to retain whatever detail may be there.

• Pseudo Skin Tones

Here's a low-tech way to give the impression of detail where little exists. This trick may be used for either wet or dry transfers, but dry works better as soaking the receptor may release some of the lightly bonded paint particles. Either way, never spray paint onto wet paper.

From about two feet away, gently spray metallic gold spray paint at the transfer paper. Don't spray evenly or thickly – you only need a little. After the paint is dry, place the exposed and imbibed carrier sheet over the painted area. Roll and separate as usual. The gold paint, when applied lightly, can act as a pseudo skin tone. However, when

"... get color corresponding to any skin or background tone."

applied too thickly, the paint will prevent the dyes from migrating to the receptor.

Silver metallic also works well with dry transfers (although the look is entirely different) but looks muddy after drying as wet transfer. Gold loses only a little of its lustre after drying. Obviously, other spray enamel colors may be tried at your discretion to get colors corresponding to any skin or background tone.

• POSTERIZATION

With wet transfers, sometimes the darkest areas do not adhere well to the receptor and may peel away when the carrier is removed. This effect, although usually unwanted, is not always unpleasant and may be enhanced by rinsing the still wet transfer under lukewarm water. When soaked, gently rub the darkest areas with a gloved finger or soft sponge. The emulsion will slowly slough away. Areas that have been de-emulsioned will still carry a light cyan color. When all dark areas are cleaned, the result can be a very nice "posterized" effect.

Fig. 7.3.: *Not all dry papers work well, but interesting results can still be attained. Type 669, Epson Card Stock.*

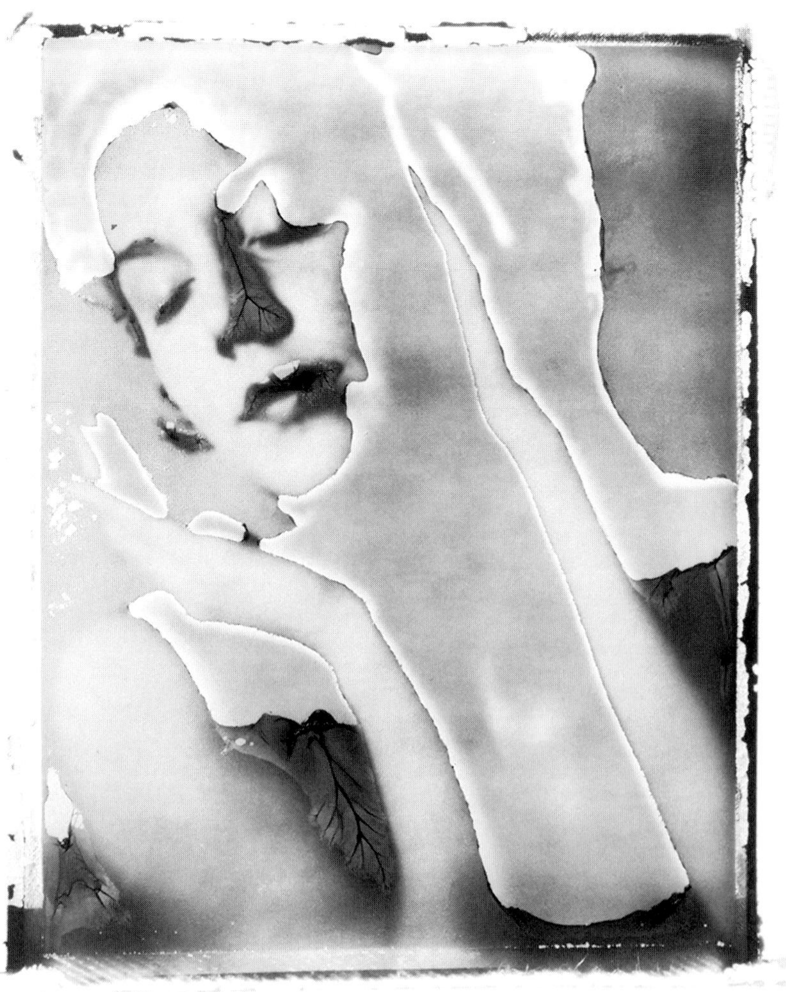

• MANIPULATE COLORS

Colors in wet transfers, while still wet, can be manipulated with watercolor paints and pigments or water soluble markers to retouch, intensify or alter transferred color. All transfers when dry will respond to reworking with colored pencils and markers. You can change, add to or subtract slightly from transfer color. Either way, you add a "plus density" because you will place color on top of color, so those areas will appear darker *(fig. 7.10)*.

• REMOVE EMULSION

Wet transfer emulsion can be gently scraped with sharp instruments or blades to alter selected areas or colors or to completely remove small areas.

• SANDPAPER AND 8X10 FILM

Using Type 809 allows you to handle the positive half of the image, as it is not light sensitive. You can create visual texture on a transfer by rubbing the surface of the positive paper with rough sandpaper or similar material. The negative will not transfer to those areas it cannot reach, so portions of the transferred image will carry no dye at all.

• ADD TEXTURE UNDER TRANSFER

For additional texture, try transferring with the carrier sheet resting on a slightly rough surface, like window screen or thick upholstery fabric. The roller will not transfer dyes evenly – some areas may not transfer at all – but the results can be very interesting.

• ADD TEXTURE OVER TRANSFER

Additional texture may be added by lightly applying a dry cloth or paper towel, or other porous material with an inherent pattern, to the finished transfer while it is still wet. The raised areas of the pattern will absorb liquid (and some color) from the receptor, resulting in a pattern within the image *(figs. 7.4-7.6)*.

"Additional texture may be added by lightly applying a dry cloth or paper towel ..."

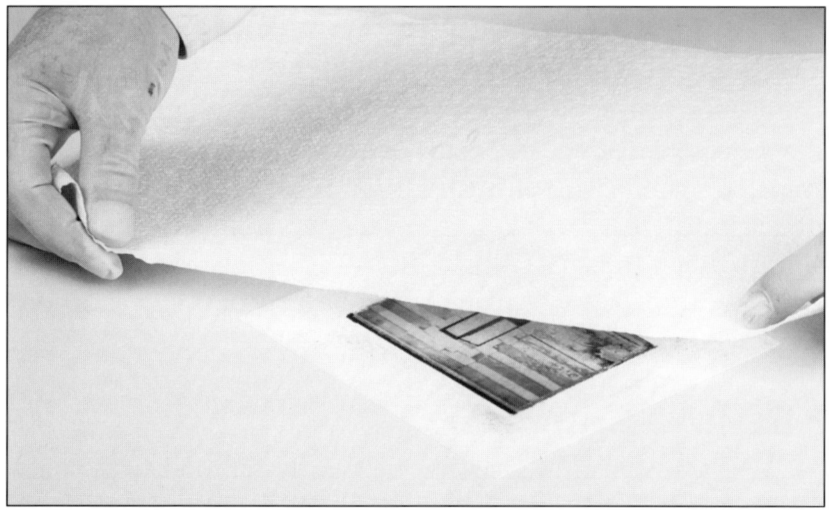

Fig. 7.4: *To add visual texture, place embossed towel or cloth onto just finished transfer.*

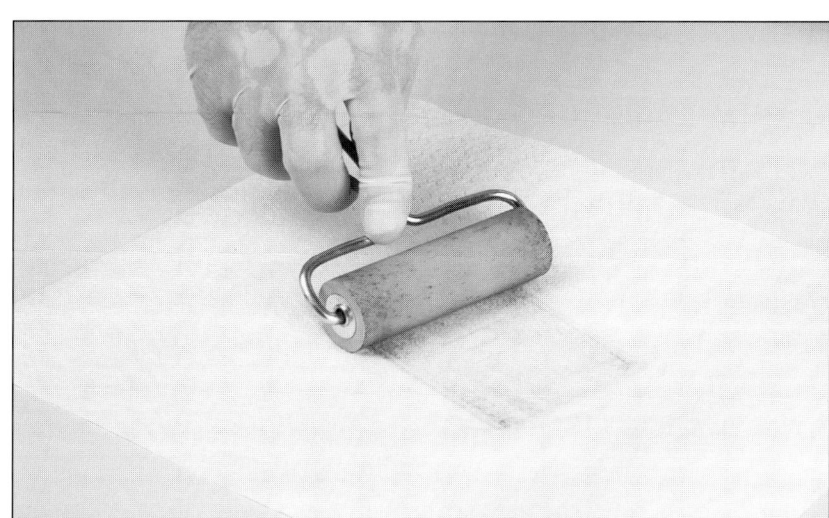

Fig. 7.5: *Gently rub over paper to transfer texture (no more than a few seconds).*

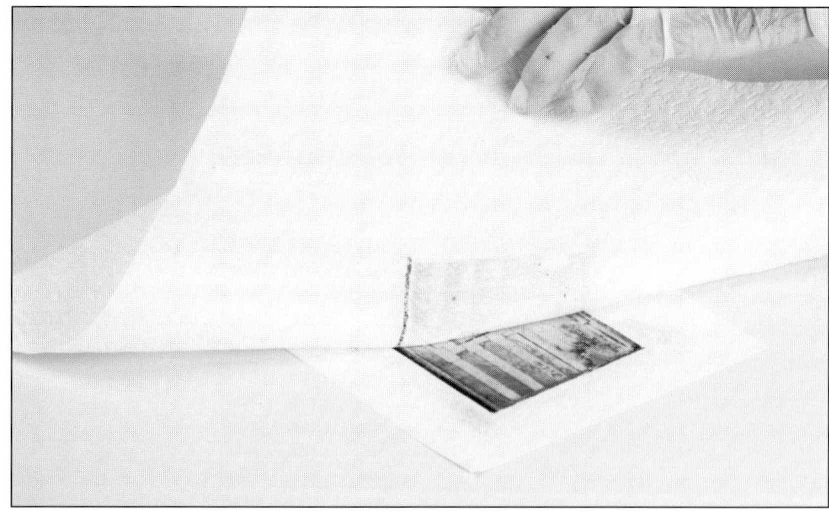

Fig. 7.6: *Remove textured paper and discard.*

• MULTIPLE TRANSFERS, SMALL AND MEDIUM FORMAT

For multiple, side-by-side transfers on one sheet of paper, lightly mark the paper for image position with a pencil before soaking *(fig.7.7)*. Don't drain the paper as much as usual and wipe off only the area ready to receive the carrier. Work from the center out, for more accurate placement. Even if you remove the film after only two minutes, it's still helpful to spray the receptor with Lysol as that keeps the paper wetter and provides a better bond.

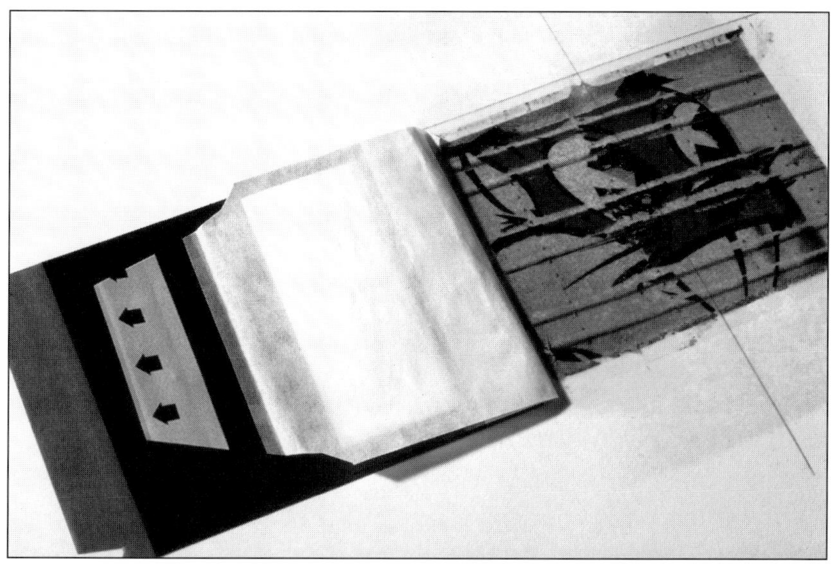

Fig. 7.7: *Draw light pencil lines to determine start points for multiple transfer. This line has been exaggerated; the actual line must be light enough to be erased after the final print is thoroughly dried.*

• MULTIPLE TRANSFERS, 8x10 MATERIAL

Arches paper may be purchased in single sheets up to 40x60 inches, but it's my understanding that only a coarse, cold press surface is available. Working with this surface is much more difficult because getting the dyes to the paper is complicated not only by the nubby texture but also by the paper's *heavy* weight. However, transfers made on this surface have a unique look to them, so if you wish to try it, here are some recommendations.

On a per-sheet basis, this paper is very expensive, so buy a corresponding sheet in a smaller size and run a number of tests on it until you are satisfied you like what's happening.

If you plan on printing side by side 8x10s, and are projection printing, first crop and make exposure calculations for the larger size, then place a Type 669 holder under the enlarger and make a test exposure. Let this develop completely to judge final color and exposure. Now make another exposure on Type 669 and test the transfer characteris-

"Plan on not answering the phone."

tics. You'll have to rub with more pressure than before, to get the dyes pushed to the base of the textured paper. Pre-spray with Lysol.

It is cheap insurance to then make an initial transfer test with a single sheet of 8x10 material.

When you're ready for the big paper, measure and mark for position with light pencil lines. Plan to work from the middle.

Be certain all materials, including the images to be exposed, are in reach, lined up in sequence and ready to go. If you have images requiring different magnifications or filtrations, make a test for each as well as a written record of exactly what you have to do. Be certain color balance and exposure are acceptable and compatible for each image.

Soak flat paper thoroughly in a clean bathtub or vertically, rolled in a container like a tall trash can.

Plan on not answering the phone. Take a deep breath and relax. You have a lot to do quickly, but if your ducks are in a row you can handle it.

When ready for the first transfer, remove the paper from its soak tray but don't overly drain it. It needs to stay wet. Keep a spray bottle of plain water as well as the Lysol near your work area. Wipe an area of the paper just slightly larger than the carrier, then spray with Lysol and wipe again. Leave everything else very wet. Imbibe and make the first transfer. Rub for two minutes, then use the spray water to re-wet any wiped edges. Leaving the first carrier in place, make the next exposure. Remove the first carrier just after placing the second, as it is then possible to accurately butt edges together.

Repeat those steps until you're finished *(fig. 7.8)*.

• OVERLAPPING TRANSFERS

To place one image within another without the "double-exposure" look, no masking is necessary. Make the first transfer and dry thoroughly. When ready for the next part, soak briefly so the paper is wet but the emulsion is still intact. Imbibe, contact and roll as usual. After the two minute minimum roll, lift the carrier and receptor and replace over several layers of paper towel. Rub for another thirty seconds to absorb water remaining in the carrier before removing to dry.

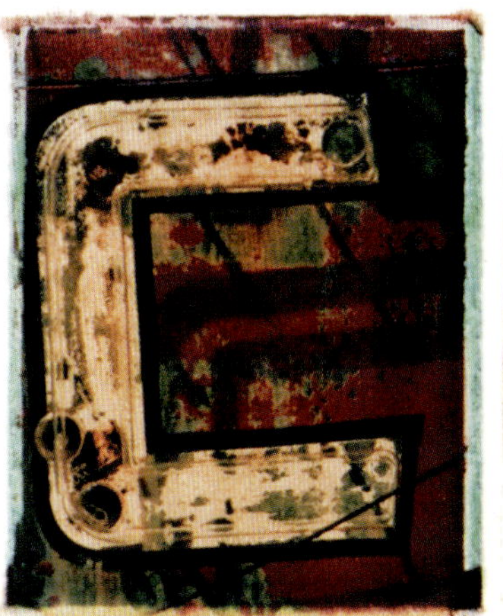
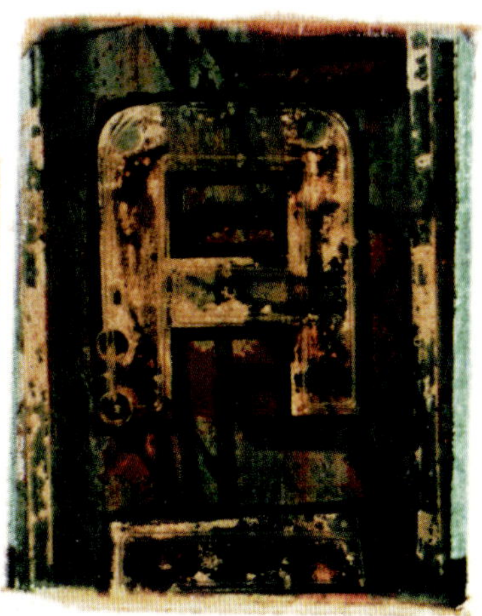
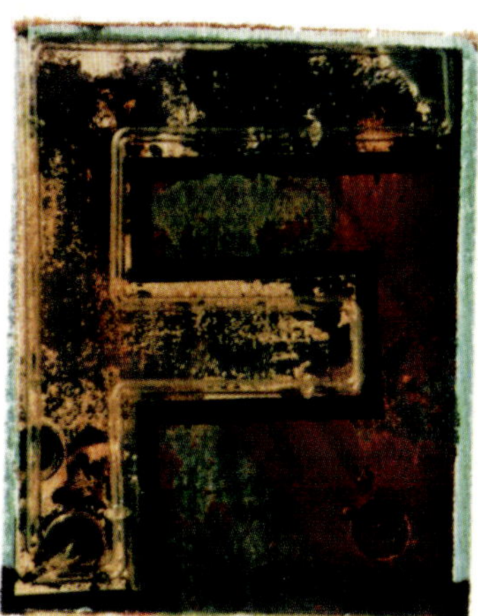
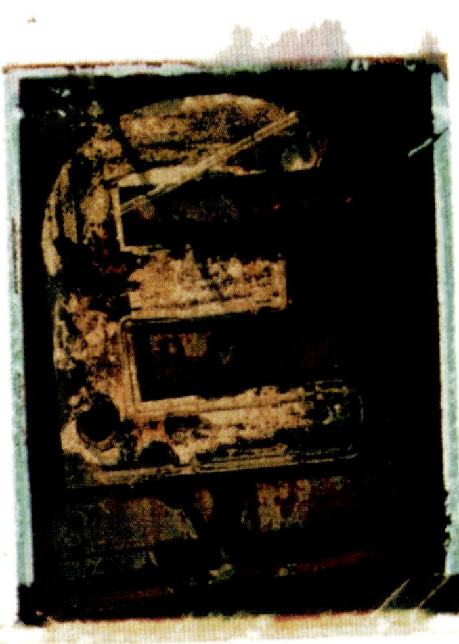

Fig. 7.8: *Side-by-side transfers may be readily accomplished with proper planning. 8x10 Type 809 images, Arches 300# Rough Surface Cold Press paper.*

• Add Color to Receptor

If you want any wet transfer to dry with an antique parchment look, soak the paper in strong, room temperature coffee prior to transfer. The effect may be lessened by mixing water with the coffee. Remove excess chemistry with a damp paper towel or place under a running tap, but be careful to not over-soak the image area. Other colors may be achieved by using red wine, food coloring, watercolor pigments or other such ingredients in the same manner.

Soaking, drying and flattening such colored papers before reuse will allow you to make dry transfers on them.

• Create Vignettes and Break Lines

To achieve a hard edge "vignette" or a clean break line somewhere within the transferred image, apply rubber cement in the pattern you wish to a sheet of dry receptor paper. Let the cement completely dry before soaking the paper and making the transfer, and let the finished transfer completely dry before picking up the rubber cement "mask" with a rubber cement eraser. If you wish to butt two images together at a clean break line, use the eraser, then mask the previously transferred side at the break line and make the second exposure after it's dry.

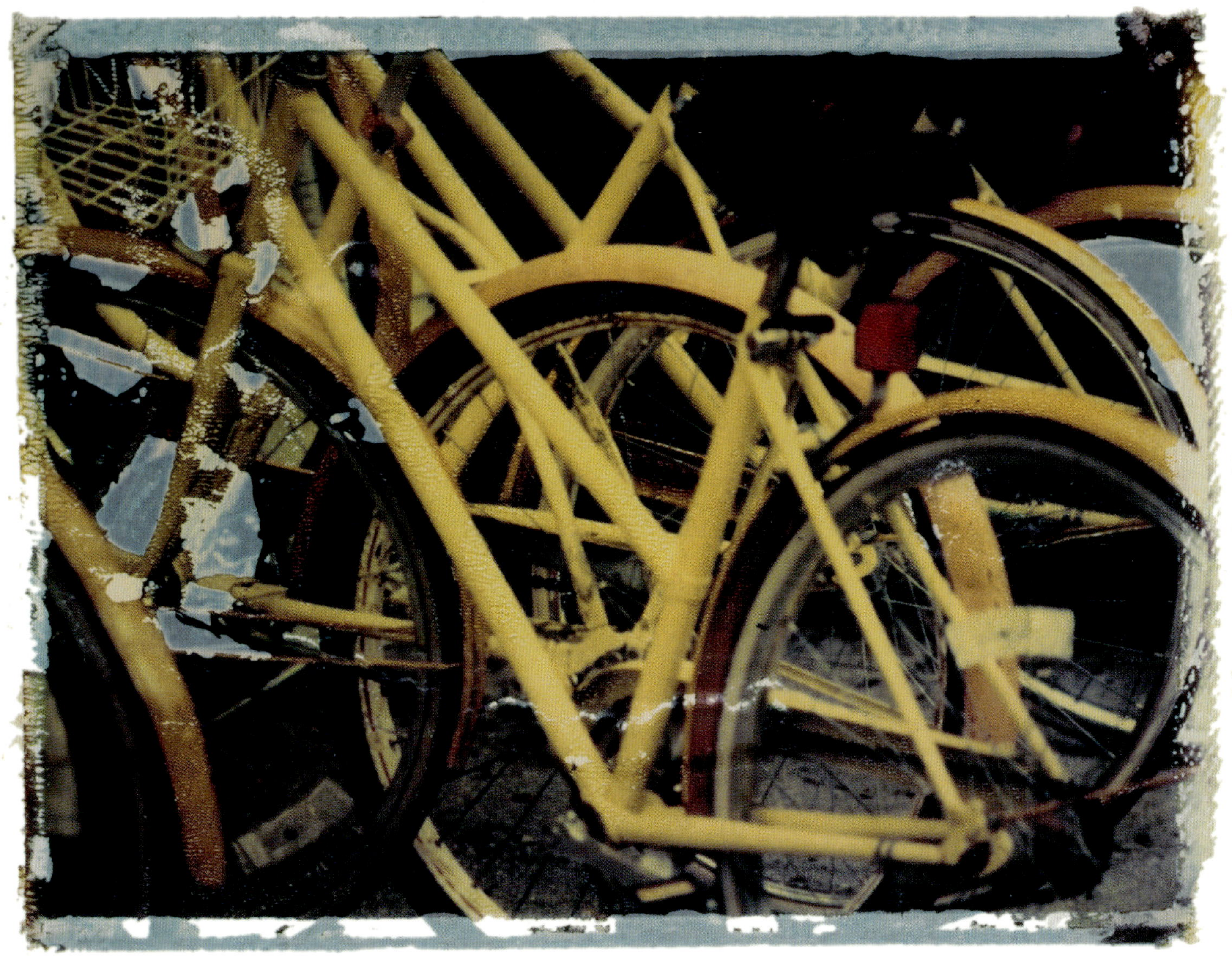

Fig. 7.9: *This paper is probably best for overall color fidelity. Areas of smooth color are unique to the dry transfer process. Type 669, Canson Air Brush Paper.*

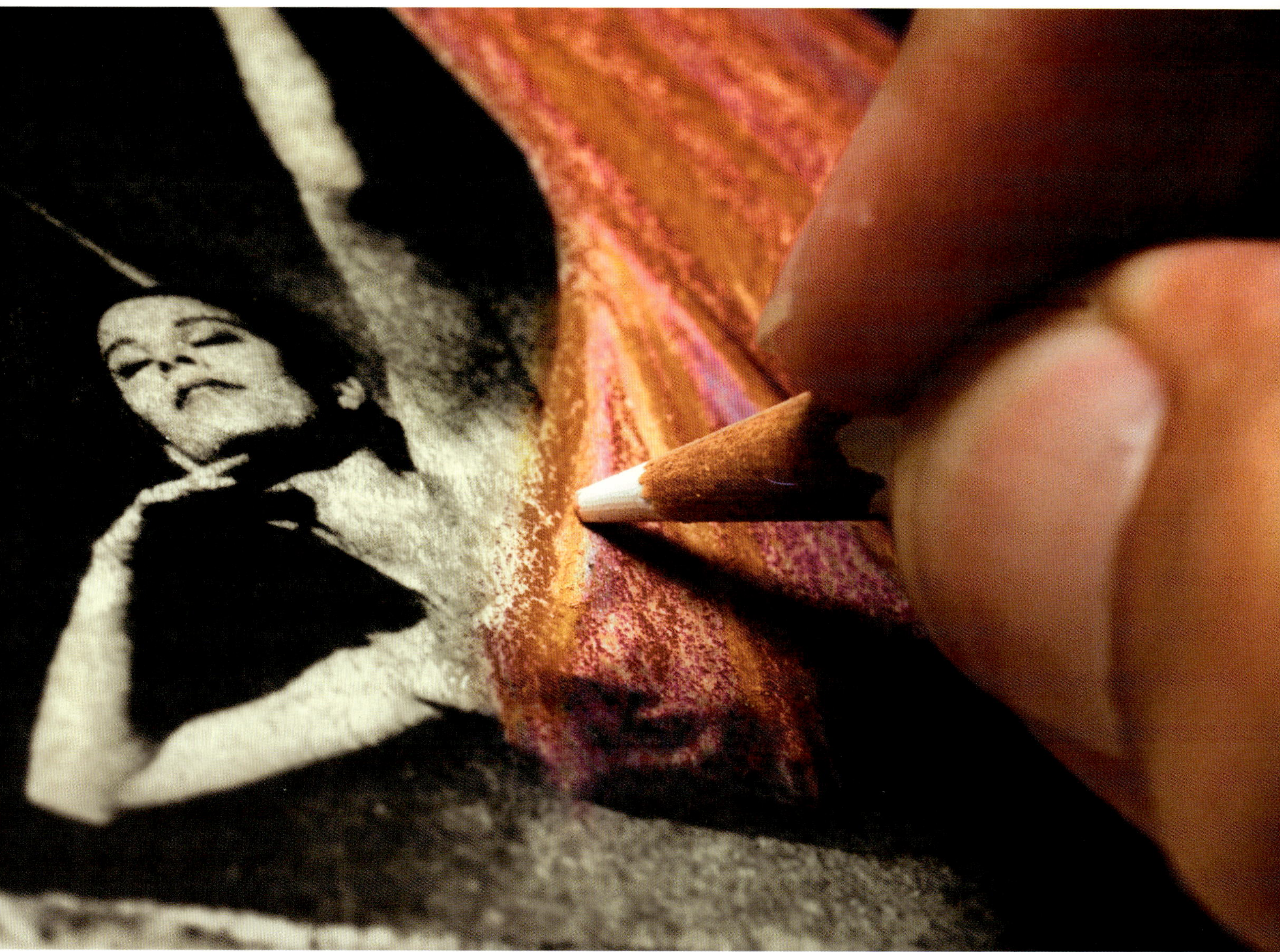

Fig. 7.10: *Image transfers on paper respond well to additional work with markers, paint or colored pencil.*

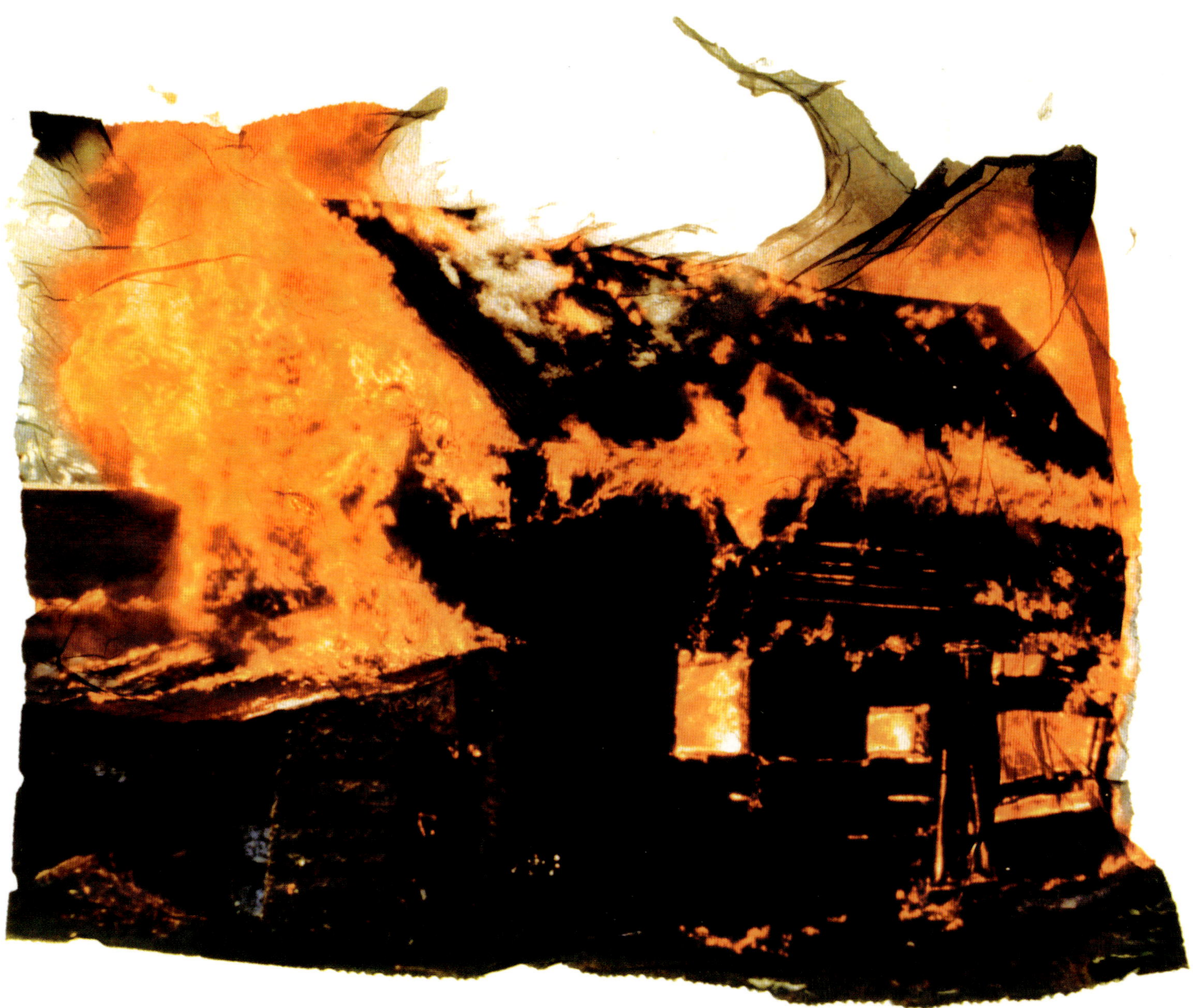

Fig. 8.1: *This print had not been thoroughly cured and began to disintegrate midway through the lift-off process. Considering the subject matter, the flaw worked very well with the image. Type 669, Arches paper.*

Chapter 8
EMULSION LIFT-OFF

• BASIC PRINCIPLES

Here's an exciting new technique that will work with many (not all – see the chart on page 8) of the Polaroid films. Essentially, this process is still an image transfer, except now you will transfer the entire, fully-developed and cured emulsion, not just the dyes *(fig. 8.1)*.

As with image transfer, the procedure for emulsion transfer is simple in theory. A finished and totally dried Polaroid print is soaked in hot water until the adhesive holding the emulsion melts away from its base. The released image is then manipulated onto another surface where it is worked into its final shape, dried, flattened and admired. However, this is not a technique for the "patience-impaired." Be prepared to spend some extra time learning the subtleties of this technique.

"... spend some extra time learning the subtleties of this technique."

• MATERIALS NEEDED

Emulsion lift-off requires more planning and additional equipment, with a few more steps before you're ready.

The materials needed for emulsion lift-off are:

- Printing method of choice
- Polaroid film of choice
- Two trays, slightly larger than working paper size
- Self-adhesive contact (shelf) paper
- Scissors or paper trimmer
- Supply of receiver paper
- Wax paper
- Hot (165-175°F or 74°-79°C) water
- Rubber surgical gloves (a must)

- Soft rubber roller
- Paper towels
- Hair dryer (optional)
- Meat or candy thermometer
- Teflon (non-stick) spatula
- X-Acto or similar graphic arts knife with fine point blade

• THE EMULSION LIFT-OFF PROCEDURE

To begin, make a print onto the selected Polaroid film via whatever method you wish. However, since you will be working in reverse, place the transparency in your equipment so the final print is "wrong-reading" or reversed according to the printer or enlarger you're using.

The print must be completely dried and "cured" before you can proceed. In real time, this means drying at room temperature for at least eight hours. You can speed up the dry time considerably by using a hair dryer against the emulsion for about three minutes on "high" at a distance of three to four inches *(fig. 8.2)*. Move the dryer in a grid motion around the print, and do not let it linger. Temperatures at the tip of most dryers are extremely hot, so watch your fingers if you're using them to anchor the print.

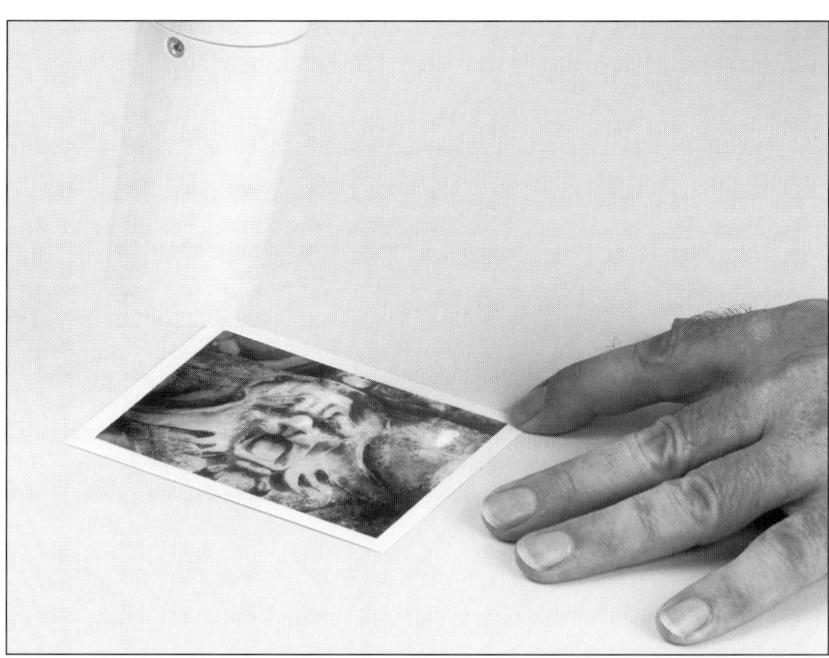

Fig. 8.2: *Thoroughly dry finished print under hot air dryer.*

Emulsions that are not completely dried and cured will be very fragile and prone to disintegrate during the process.

After the print is thoroughly dry, cut a piece of self-adhesive contact paper slightly larger than the print. Expose the adhesive and, with the print face down on a clean flat work surface, adhere the paper to the back of the print *(fig. 8.3)*. Use the roller to remove any bubbles that may occur in the placement and to tighten the bond between the surfaces *(fig. 8.4)*. If you get a crease in the contact paper, the adhesive is not very strong, and you can easily peel it up and start over. It's necessary to seal the backs of Polaroid prints because the material has a white plastic backing that melts

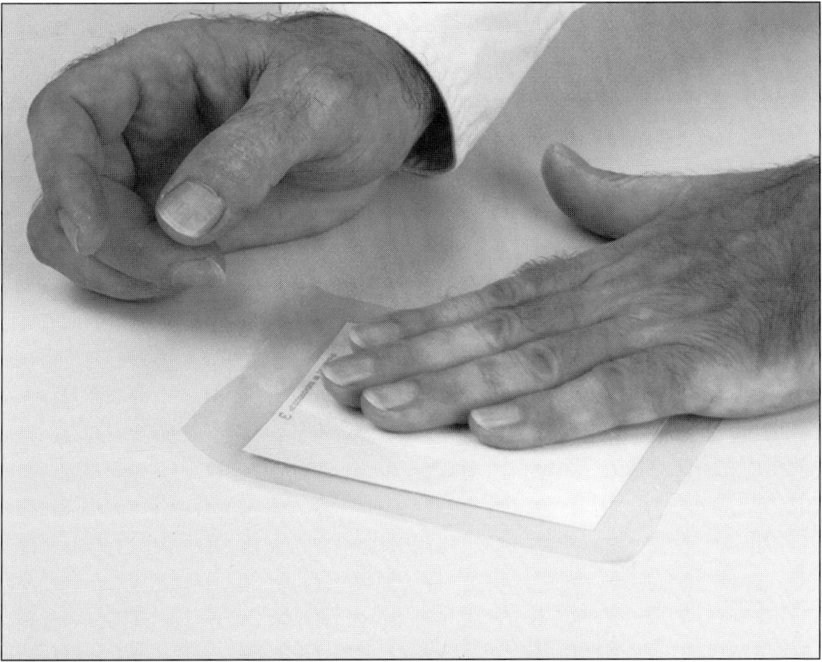

Fig. 8.3: *Place contact paper over back of print.*

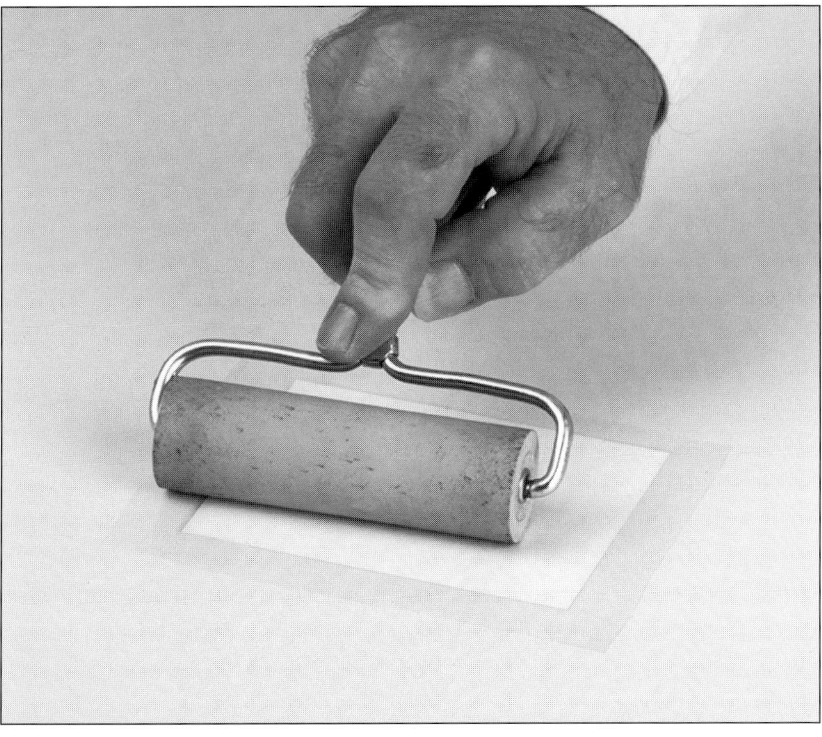

Fig. 8.4: *Strengthen bond of contact paper to print back with roller.*

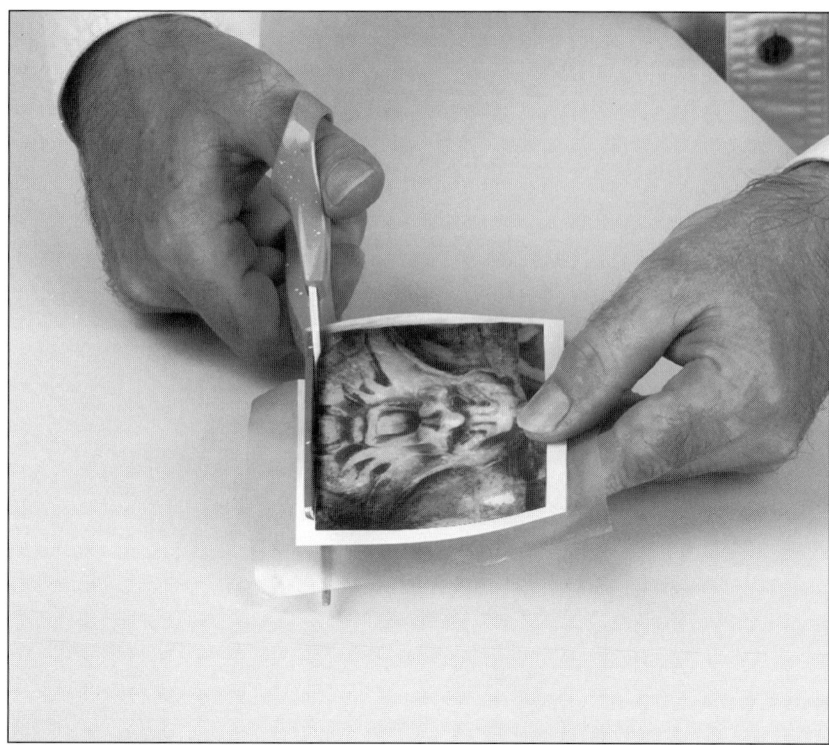

Fig. 8.5: *Cut away print borders.*

at a lower temperature than the emulsion. If not sealed it will discolor the water bath, get on the surface of your print and all over your fingers and equipment.

With the scissors or a paper trimmer, trim off the white border around the print *(figs. 8.5)*. This is the area of strongest bond between the emulsion and the base. Trimming just slightly into the print area guarantees the hot water will find its way under the emulsion.

"An instructor I know uses a portable tea brewer as his source of hot water ..."

Very few taps dispense hot water at 165°-175°F (74°-79°C), and you will need a stable supply of it for this step to work properly. You may use a standard sauce pan or tea kettle, heating the water and monitoring with a thermometer, adding cold water if necessary. An instructor I know uses a portable tea brewer as his source of hot water whenever he demonstrates the lift-off process. The brewer's temperature is easy to regulate and it heats about a pint of water to the desired temperature in just a few minutes. Both of these methods require replenishment of hot water on a per-print basis.

My thrift store skillet will maintain a selected temperature as long as the water lasts and has a 12"x12" base, large enough for an 8"x10" print. Once the optimum temperature was determined with a thermometer, I simply taped the thermostat in place, assuring correct and constant temperature whenever I use it.

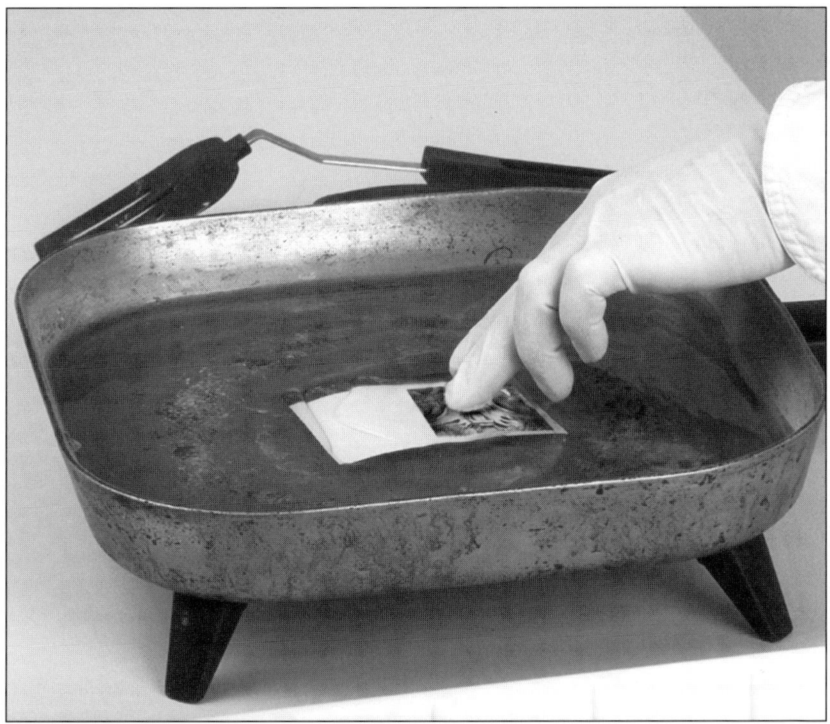

Fig. 8.6: *Place in scalding hot water. Personal contact is at your discretion but must be brief.*

When the water is correct and the print back is sealed, you may submerge the print, face up, in the hot water. Although any caustic chemistry has long dried, you still need to wear at least one rubber surgical glove. The glove acts like a heat-transfer device, keeping most of the heat away from your skin for short (only a second or two) periods of time, but allows you to use your fingers to submerge and manipulate the print. The water is hot, and can easily cause scalding burns if you leave your fingers in too long. *Be careful.* By using your gloved fingertip to push the print into the water, you will lessen the chance of damaging the emulsion with a sharp fingernail or utensil. After submersion, gently rock the water to keep a steady supply of hot water flowing over the entire surface *(fig 8.6).*

"... gently rock the water to keep a steady supply of hot water flowing over the entire surface."

Depending on the emulsion, it usually takes at least four minutes for the base under the image to melt enough for the image to begin to lift-off. Do not let the image completely disengage from the base; it will float away and you will have trouble getting it out of the hot water in one piece. Ideally, you should let about 75% of the emulsion release before removing the image from the hot water.

When removing the print *(fig. 8.7)*, do not grab the emulsion with your fingers or trap it against a utensil – it may rip. The Teflon spatula is invaluable for removing the print, as you can easily get under the melting material. Slide the spatula under the print, lifting and draining once the

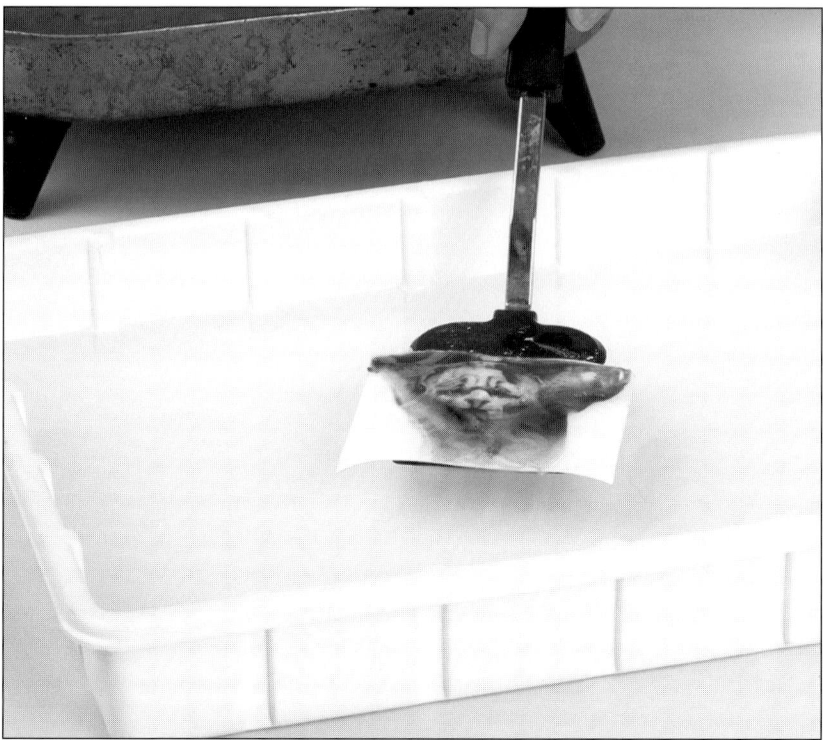

Fig. 8.7: *Remove from hot water when emulsion is 75% free.*

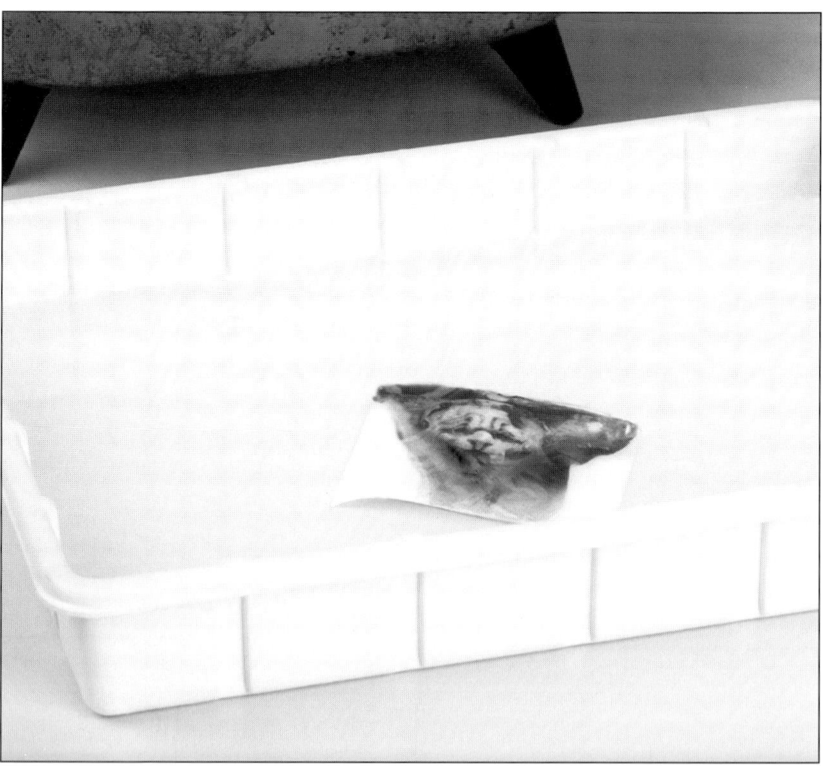

Fig. 8.8: *Place in second tray and agitate until emulsion floats off base. Discard base.*

QUICK TIPS:

If you are doing lift-offs from "live" shoots, or from images that have been printed "right-reading," put the wax paper back into the water face down, and release the emulsion. Now slide the wax paper back under it, and remove it again. This insures the image will be "right-reading" when finally transferred.

print is centered on it. Let the water drain over the sides, and do not allow the loose emulsion to overhang the base edges by more that a few millimeters (it may stretch). Immediately place it, still emulsion up, in the tray of cold water (tap water – cold, even tepid – is fine), and gently rock the tray to dislodge the remaining attached emulsion *(fig. 8.8)*. When it floats away freely, remove the base paper and discard.

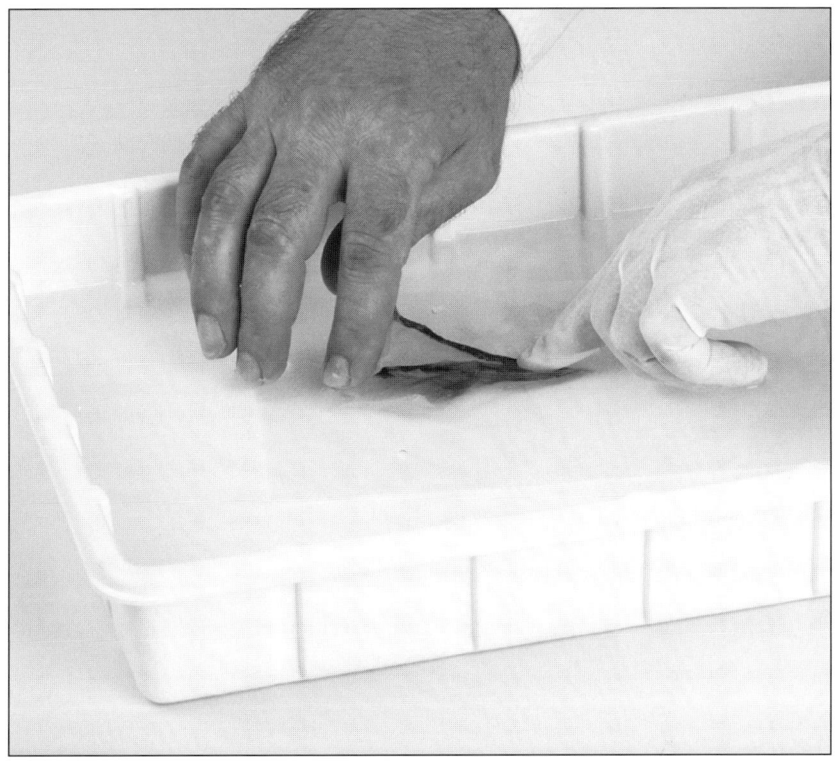

Fig. 8.9: *Gently uncurl the emulsion.*

This next step is the trickiest, and although it may seem like trying to untangle a jellyfish, it can be done easily if you're patient.

"... it may seem like trying to untangle a jellyfish..."

Take a piece of wax paper, about twice the size of your print, and slide it under the emulsion. Wax paper will float, and will bring the emulsion up with it. *Gently* (I can't stress that enough) work any kinks out of the emulsion, using the tip of a gloved finger and the action of the water *(fig. 8.9)*. Whenever possible, avoid touching the emulsion with your fingers – let the water do the work.

When you have the loose emulsion relatively flat, gently hold in place with fingertips on two corners and remove the wax paper and the emulsion from the water. Set it aside.

Take the receptor paper and place it in the water. Paper does not have to be thoroughly soaked, just wet enough so the emulsion can be manipulated without sticking. Lift the paper from the tray and drain for about ten seconds, then place it on a flat, waterproof work surface. Almost any paper will do, provided it can withstand immersion in water.

Now take the wax paper with the emulsion and hold it over the receptor. Get it close enough so you can gauge the

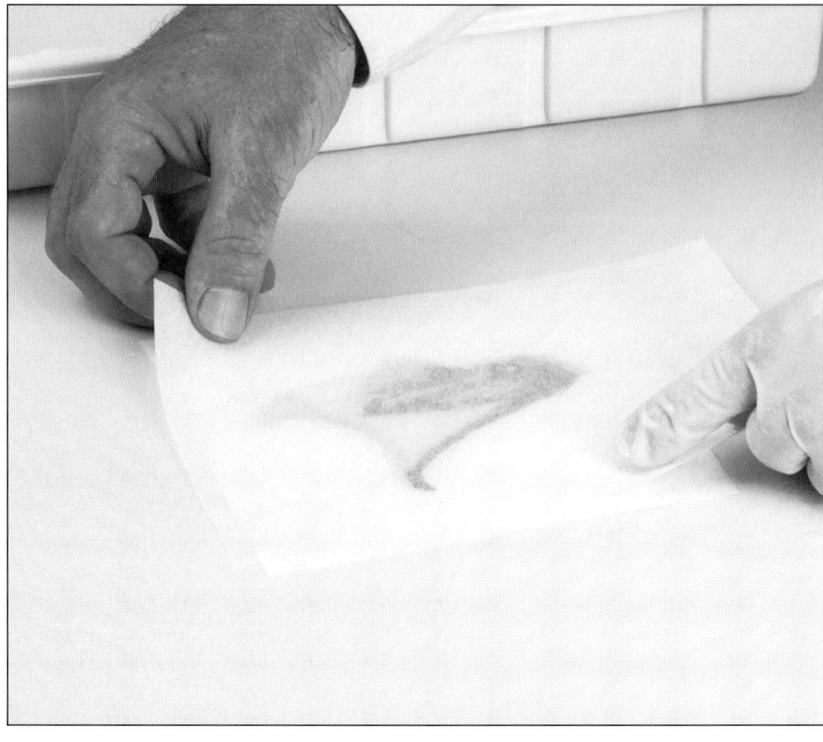

Fig. 8.10: *Slide onto wax paper or dry mount tissue and place, face down, loosely on final receptor.*

"... manipulate the creases and borders for artistic effect ..."

final position of the image, then make contact between the surfaces. Use your roller and lightly press the back of the wax paper behind the entire image to adhere the emulsion to the paper. Press a fingertip from the back onto one corner, to guarantee adhesion, then slowly peel the wax paper away from the receiving paper *(fig. 8.10)*.

After the paper with the emulsion has been removed from the water, the image position may be finessed further. Take the receiving sheet and immerse the image at an angle until about half covered. Using back-and-forth and/or dip-and-dunk motions in the water, either work the emulsion kinks out or put more in. Don't put the entire receiving sheet under water at one time or the emulsion will float off and you'll have to start the placement procedure again.

When the emulsion is in place and you like its design, drain the paper for at least ten seconds and then place it on the work surface. You will now use the roller to press the image into the pores of the paper and establish the bond.

Wet the roller in the soak tray before starting, then place the roller in the center of the image and lightly roll to the edges *(fig. 8.11)*. This insures that the emulsion will not stick to the dry rubber. You will find you can further manipulate the creases and borders for artistic effect by varying the pressure and direction of the roller.

I've found it helpful to place finished but still wet lift-offs on cloth or paper towels to draw excess water away

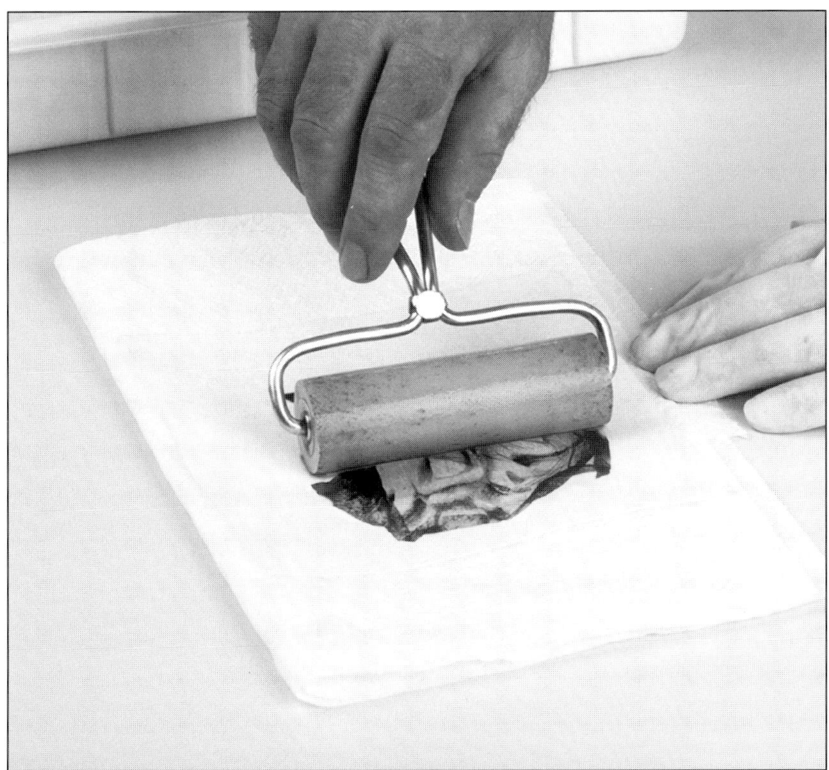

Fig. 8.11: *With a wet roller, begin at center and roll past paper edges to blot excess water.*

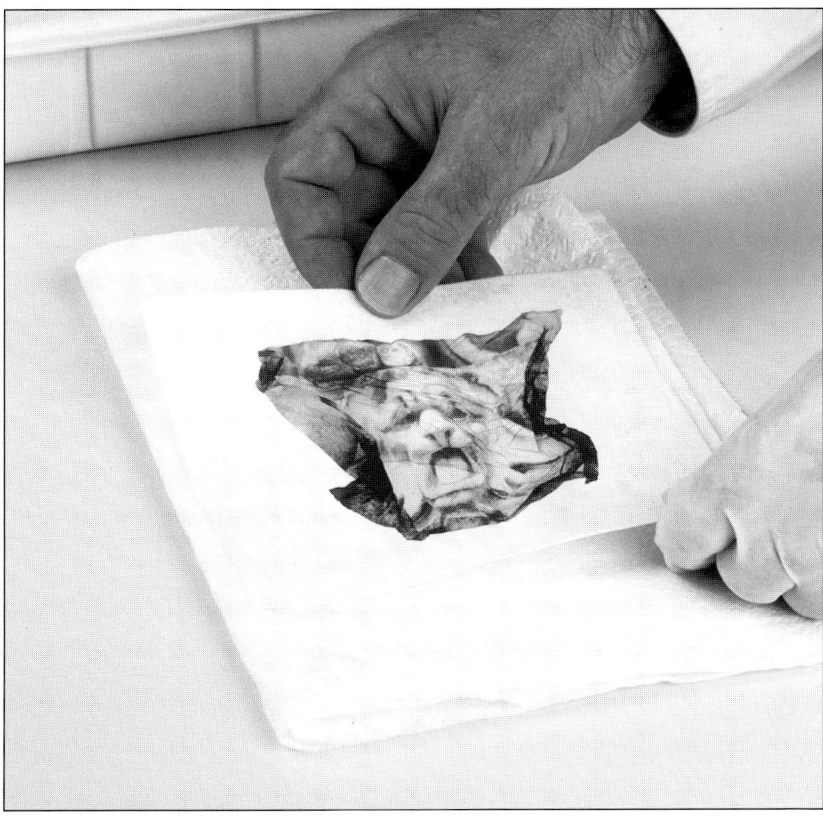

Fig. 8.12: *Place formed lift-off on several sheets of paper towel.*

from the emulsion *(fig. 8.12)*. If your paper is too wet, areas of emulsion that overlap on the print may not properly bond to themselves and will rise away from the paper as they dry. Raised areas of dry emulsion are quite brittle and will readily chip away with any abrasive or rough handling. Drying time can be decreased by aiming a small fan at the wet papers. Low speed will do nicely; you just need to move air over the surfaces.

"Any clear spray will help the dry emulsion stay on the paper ..."

Dry, curly prints may be flattened in a dry mount press set on low (180°) for approximately two minutes. You may also use a clothes iron, low heat, no steam.

After drying and flattening, spray finished lift-offs with a clear acrylic spray such as Krylon Crystal Clear or Matte Finish, or a Marshall's UV protective spray. Any clear spray will help the dry emulsion stay on the paper and protect the surface; UV spray will help protect the dyes from fading.

Chapter 9

TRICKS AND TIPS FOR EMULSION LIFT-OFF

• LIFT-OFFS AND OTHER SURFACES

You can transfer an emulsion to an almost unlimited number of surfaces. Frosted glass, acetate, wood, plaster and cloth are just a few *(fig. 9.1)*. As the emulsion you are transferring has limited stretching capability, be careful that its new base will not be drastically flexed. This would cause the emulsion to crack and fall away. Before transferring to new cloth, be certain to wash out any sizing.

"You can transfer an emulsion to an almost unlimited number of surfaces."

• WAX PAPER ALTERNATIVE

Wax paper is the easiest assist paper to find, but not the easiest to use. It will get waterlogged and shred a bit after a while, and it is sometimes difficult to keep flat when moving the emulsion onto it. Some artists use clear acetate because it's waterproof and stiff, but it curls when wet. The best surface I've found so far is drymount tissue. It's both stiff and flexible enough to work with and does not get waterlogged. One piece, carefully used, could last a lifetime.

• OVERALL COLOR

Because the emulsion is not opaque, you can change the overall color of an image by placing it on off-white or colored paper.

• CUTTING & REPOSITIONING ONTO COLORED BACKGROUNDS

If you wish to show an image with a white background against a colored field, first make the lift-off onto a brilliant or bright white 100% cotton stationery. After drying and

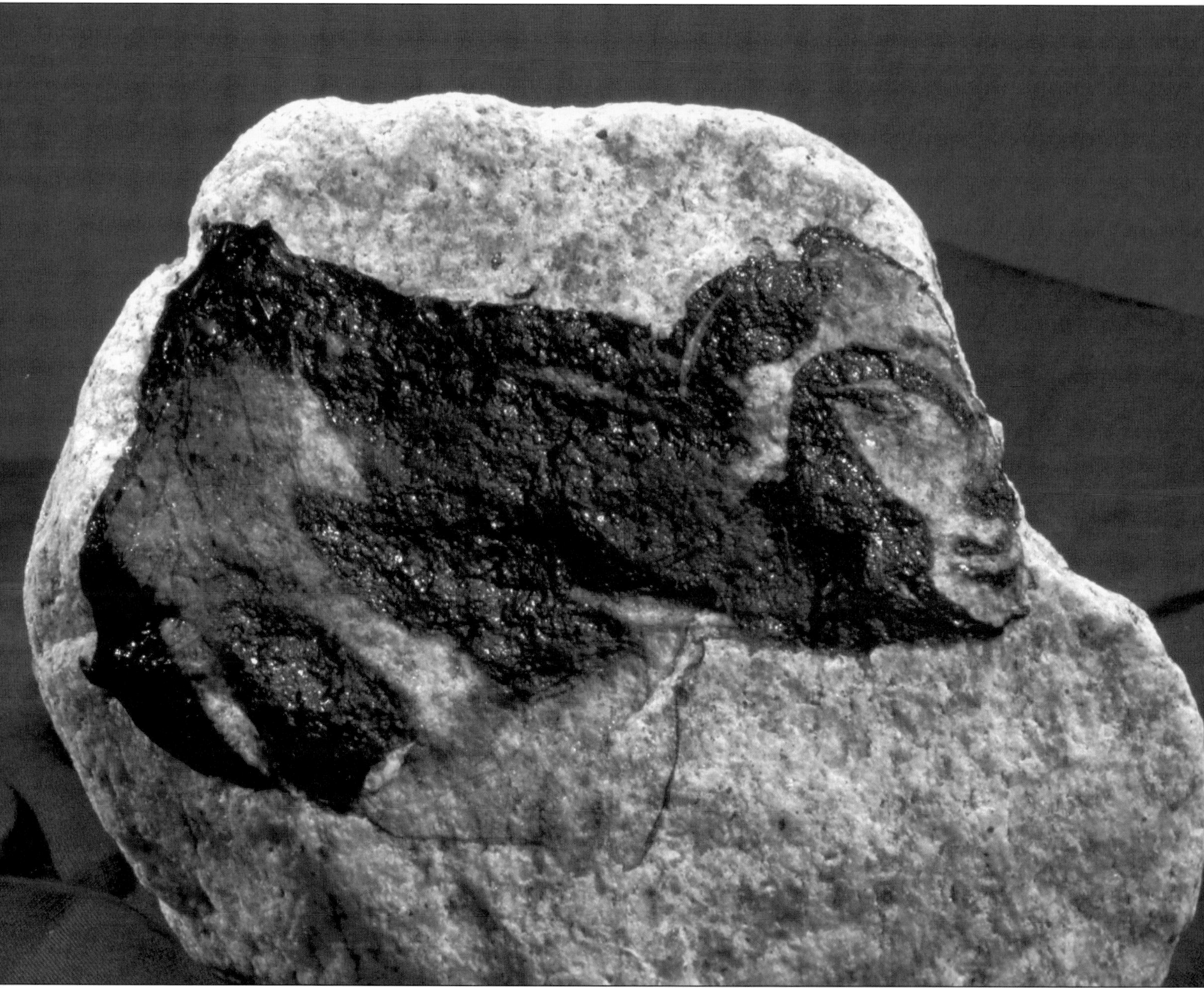

Fig. 9.1: *Emulsion transfers are easily accomplished onto rough surfaces like clean rock.*

flattening, carefully cut around with edges with an X-Acto knife. Then spray mount that image onto a base of another color. Stationery with an embossed finish, such as Classic Laid linen, will allow some of its pattern to show through under the emulsion *(fig. 9.4)*.

• Outline Images

You can "outline" or isolate areas of the image by lightly cutting around their edges with an X-Acto knife *(fig. 9.5)*. You never need to cut all the way through the base, just through the thin emulsion layer. After you've moved the partially released emulsion to the cold water, break the line separating the two pieces with a finger and swirl the unwanted emulsion onto it, then discard.

• PROBLEM WITH CLOSE-DATED FILM

Sometimes, when using film that is close to its expiration date, the emulsion will be much harder to remove, no matter how long you leave it in the hot water. This problem is usually recognized when hot emulsion bubbles up from the middle of the picture, rather from the sides. Over-soaking in hot water will eventually weaken the emulsion, making it prone to tears, so you'll want to get it into the cold water as soon as a side loosens. Using a gloved finger, you can carefully and gently push the emulsion away from the base. You may encounter some areas that just don't want to move. Try replacing that part of the image in the hot water, and agitating gently until it finally loosens.

"This problem is usually recognized when hot emulsion bubbles up from the middle of the picture ..."

• REPAIR SMALL HOLES

Small tears and rips can sometimes be repaired by carefully moving the damaged bits of emulsion back into place while the image is still wet. Small tears and rips can easily be hidden after the print is dry by using watercolor or spotting dyes *(fig. 9.2)*.

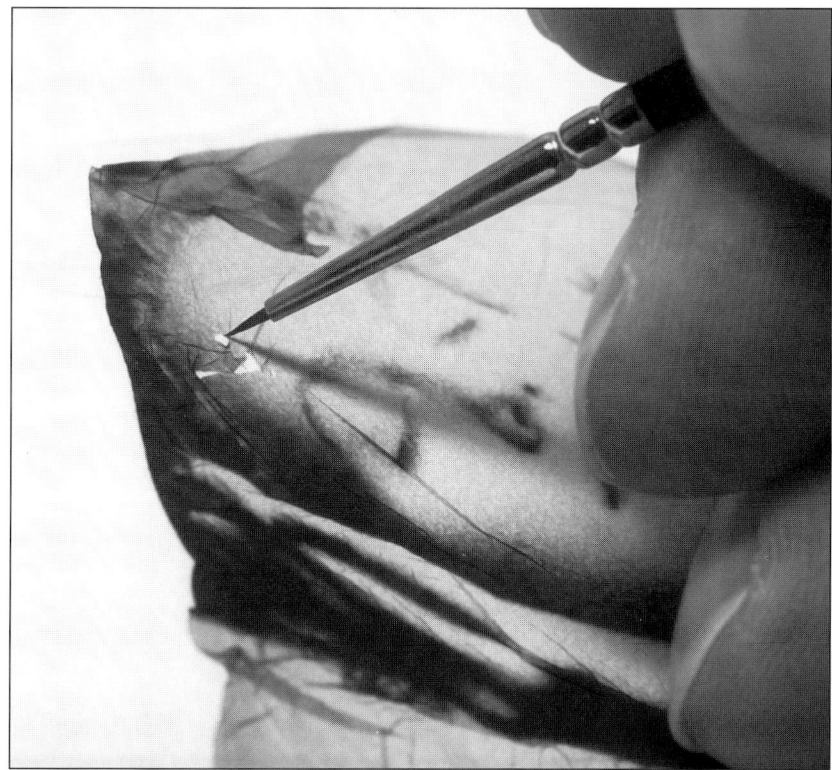

Fig. 9.2: *Small rips may be easily hidden by using retouching fluid or watercolors and a retouching brush.*

• REPAIR LARGE HOLES

If you're making several lift-offs of the same image and you accidentally ruin one, keep it moist on its own piece of wax paper or dry mount tissue. You can cut small pieces out with your knife, and use them to repair rips or tears in other prints. After you cut the patch, lift it just enough to work a smooth edged painter's spatula under it. Lift it off on the spatula and move it over the area to be filled (ideally, you'll want a patch slightly larger that the hole you're filling). Holding it in position with one hand, drop water from an eye dropper down the spatula surface but behind the trailing edge of the patch and "float" it into place. You can move it a bit with a gloved finger after it's down, but it will be fragile. To lock it into place, dry that area slightly with a hair dryer.

• UNIQUE CORNERS

"... give your corners a unique look ..."

If you'd like to give your corners a unique look, you can do so after the emulsion is in place but before it's been rubbed down. First, blot the area around the corner with a paper towel. Be careful not to touch the emulsion. With a dry rubber roller, start just outside the corner and roll across it. The emulsion will stick to the roller and roll off with it. After rolling $^1/_2$" to $^3/_4$" further, pick up the roller just enough to clear the paper and turn it slightly in whatever direction you wish to go, or move it slightly forward, in the direction of the roll, then put it back on the paper and reverse the roll. Finish the rub by wetting the roller and starting from the middle. If you don't like it, you can either redo the roll, or put that corner back into the cold water and move it back to its previous position.

• IMAGES LOOK BRIGHTER

To make your final images appear brighter than they actually are, frame with a mat cut from slightly off-white rag mat board. On first inspection, most people perceive the larger, off-white area, as pure white, and will subconsciously see the image as extremely bright.

• IMAGES FOR TRANSFER AND LIFT-OFF

You can make some Polaroid photographs do double duty, producing both an image transfer and emulsion lift-off from the same two pieces of material. A thirty second imbibe time will often produce a print with a full complement of colors, although they will be slightly muted and on the pastel side. Make the image transfer as you normally would but save the print. After it's fully cured you can use it to make an emulsion lift-off.

• MOUNTING MULTIPLE IMAGES

You may mount images side by side on one sheet of receptor paper. After the first is done and rolled into final position, re-wet the receptor up to the edge of the first emulsion. Float the new lift-off emulsion onto the receptor and position to your taste. Repeat with as many new pieces as you wish. Be careful that the first do not overly dry, or those emulsions, their bonds loosened by continued movement and drying at a different rate than the paper, could get brittle enough to pop off.

"You may mount images side by side on one sheet of receptor paper."

• MIRROR IMAGES

Similarly, you can mount mirror images by making two identical prints and simply flopping one of the emulsions to "wrong reading" when in the cold water tray *(fig. 9.3)*. Any differences in surface reflectivity or visual texture will be hidden after the dried piece has been sprayed with acrylic.

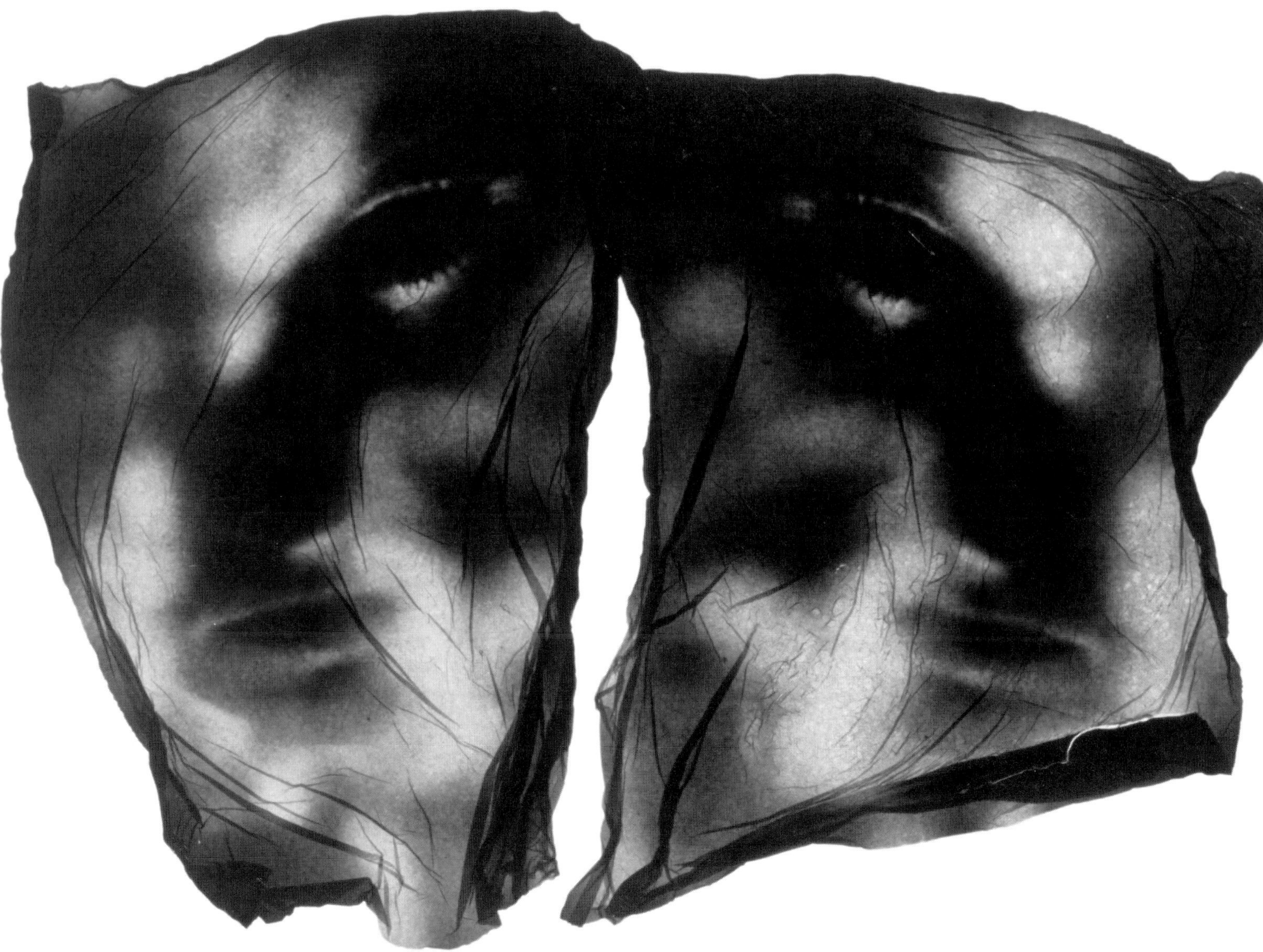

Fig. 9.3: *One of the identical images was flopped before placement. Type 669, Strathmore paper.*

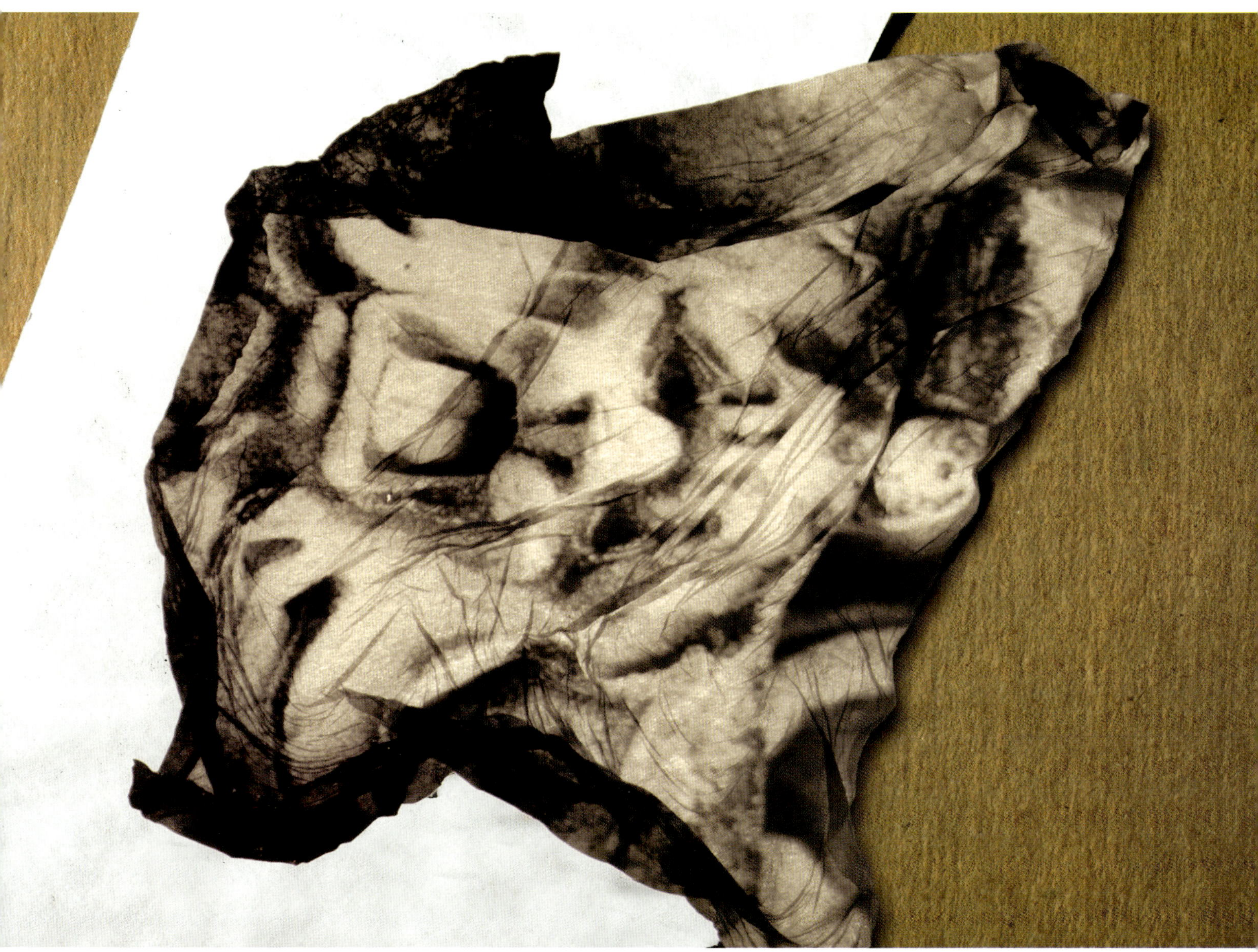

Fig. 9.4: *It's easy to dry an emulsion transfer onto bright, white paper. When dry, cut the image with a utility knife and reposition the transfer onto colored paper stock.*

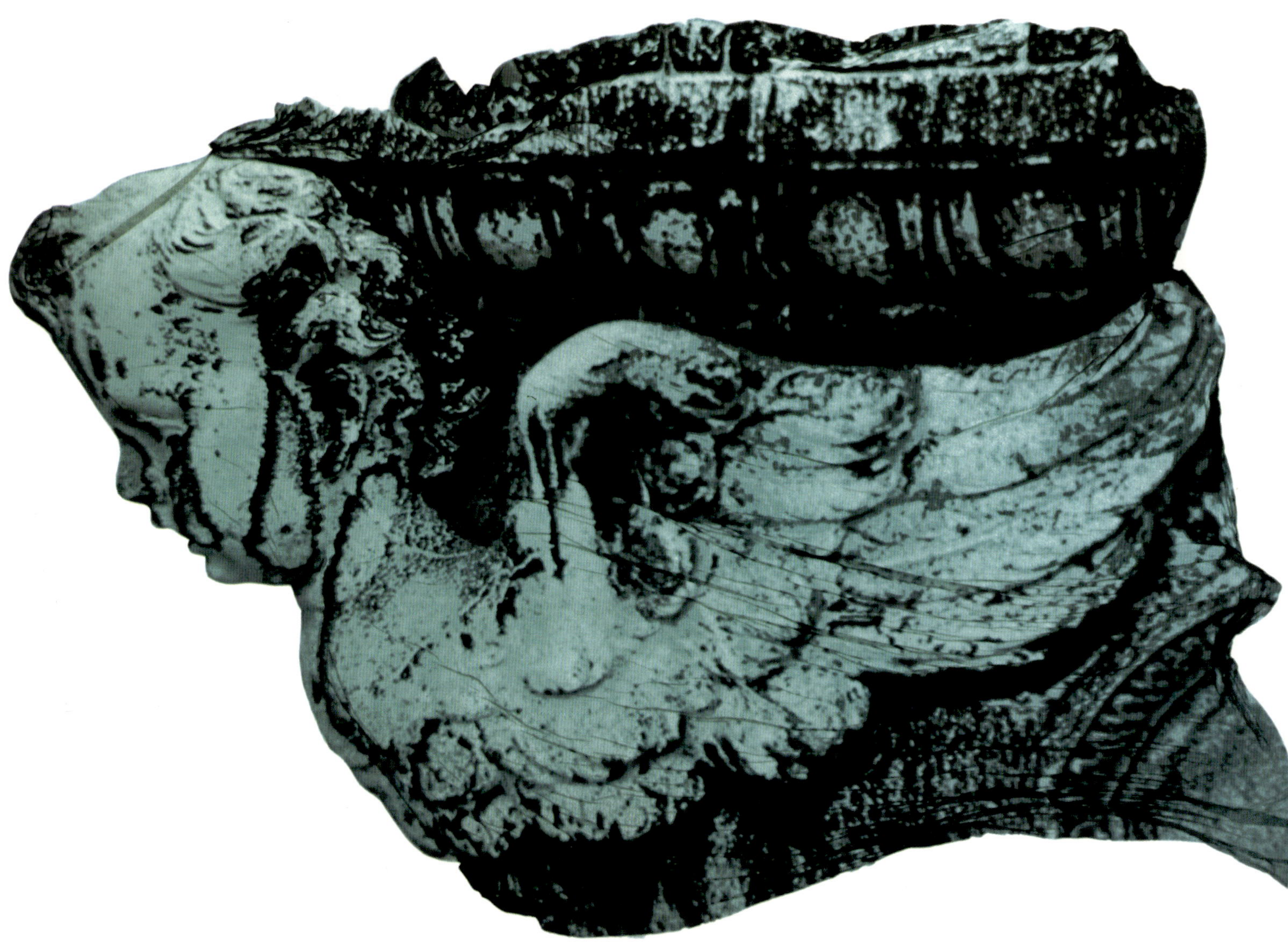

Fig. 9.5: *Lift-off images may be outlined by lightly cutting the emulsion with a graphic arts knife prior to water immersion. Do not cut through the print back.*

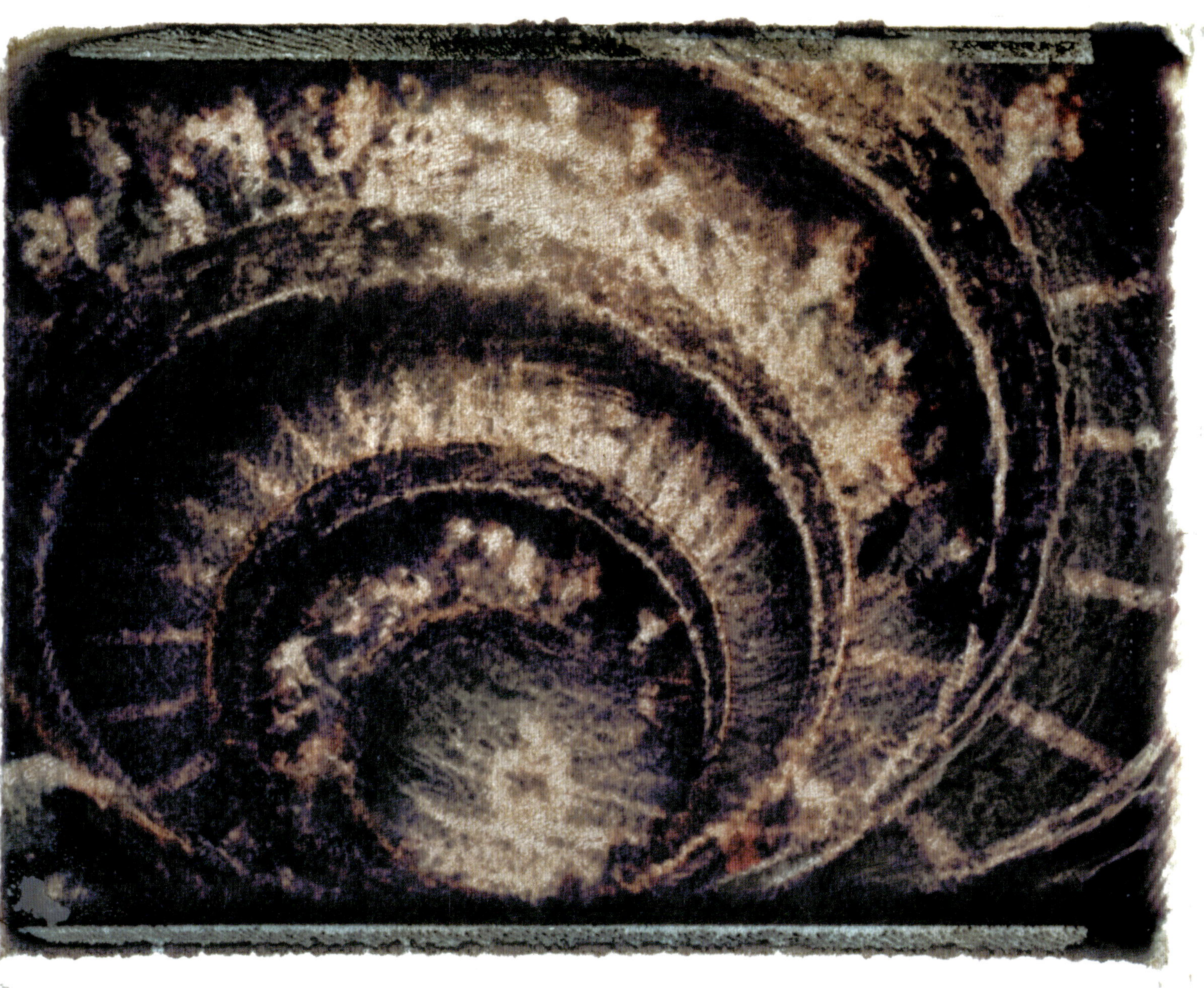

Fig. 10.1: *Printing through a glass covered with petroleum jelly will produce an Impressionistic image by bending the projected light.*

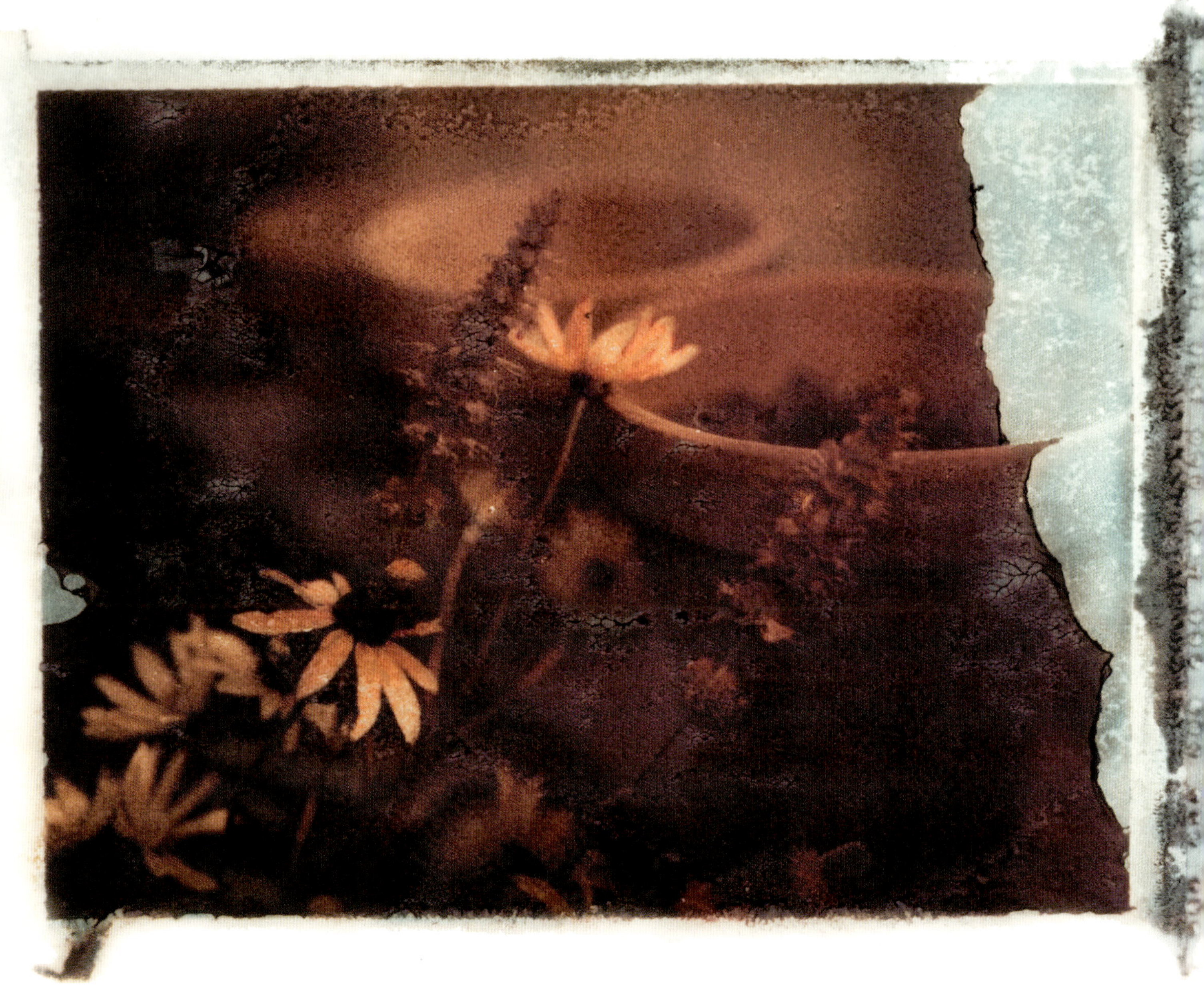

fig. 10.2: *Live transfer made in the field. 4x5 Type 59, Arches paper.*

Chapter 10

PRINTING TECHNIQUES

• POPULAR PRINTING EQUIPMENT

There are a number of methods one might use to get an image onto Polaroid film. The easy, versatile machines described here represent state-of-the-art Polaroid printing technology.

"... the automatic exposure sensor guarantees precise prints and transfers ..."

• THE DAYLAB II SLIDE PRINTER

Here's a machine that does it all. Through a simple yet ingenious modular system of bases which attach to a color-head printer, this printer allows you to make transfers to any size Polaroid material, pack-size through 8x10 *(fig. 10.3)*.

The machine features a series of exposure settings that, once set for your preferences, remain constant. Easy to note in increments of five color correction points, you can readily reposition the controls to accommodate any film type or preference change. Built-in yellow-magenta-cyan dichroic filtration allows an almost infinite variety of color changes, and permits a degree of fine tuning previously rivaled only by projection printing in the darkroom. Best of all, the automatic exposure sensor guarantees precise prints and transfers, based on your previously noted preferences or changes made as you work.

Here's how it works. You choose the appropriate base for the film size you wish to use, and attach it below the printing tower. All film sizes have a dedicated base, so you are able to purchase only those that apply to your work. The bases are attached by simply placing the printing tower over the plastic insets molded into the base itself.

The 35mm slide (you may also use the outdated 127 "Super Slide") is placed into a plastic carrier, and slid into

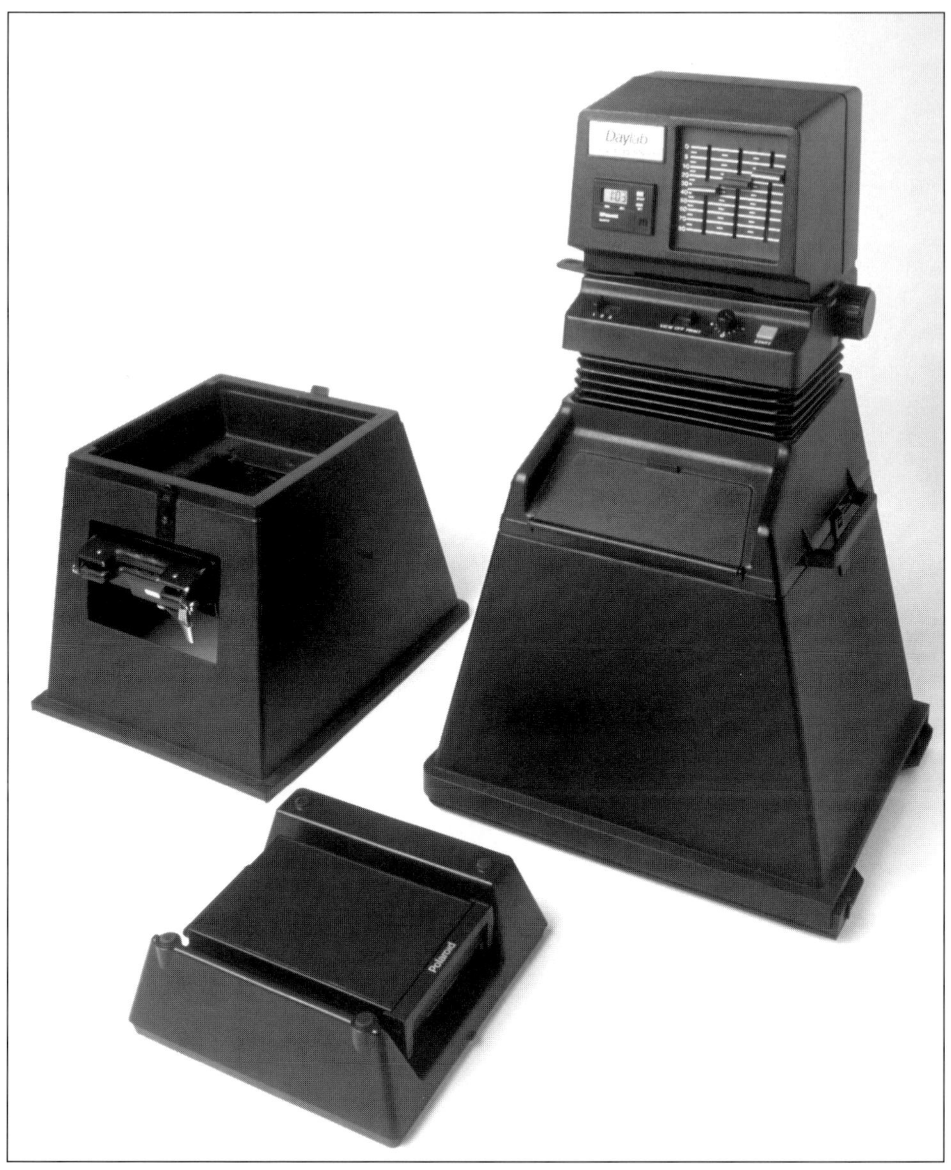

Fig. 10.3: *The DayLab II printer on the 8x10 modular base, shown alongside the 4x5 and pack size bases.*

place below the enlarging lens. Turning a knob on one side of the machine raises or lowers the enlarging head, to increase or decrease the degree of enlargement. Fine tuning the same knob allows for fine focus (not possible with any other copy method except projection printing). Cropping and enlargement are fine tuned under white light while viewing through a closeable "window" in the tower, the image projecting against the white guide board that covers the film holder *(fig. 10.4)*.

After you have cropped the image to your satisfaction, close the window, pull out the white focus card, turn off the "view" light and switch the selector to "print". Gently push the button when ready. When the exposing light clicks off, replace the white card, pull the Polaroid film and begin the imbibe time and transfer process.

All remaining steps to transfer or lift-off have been fully explained in the previous chapters.

You may have to make a few fully developed Polaroid prints before you are satisfied the automatic settings default to your preferences. This is very easy, especially if you make notes as you go. Should you decide exposure is correct, but overall color needs some tweaking, the color head will easily take care of that while making any necessary exposure changes by adding or subtracting color via the built-in yellow, magenta and cyan filters *(fig. 10.5)*.

• THE DAYLAB JUNIOR

A smaller version of the above, this machine is fixed focus and accepts only pack films, for which the base is permanently attached. It does have the same dichroic color

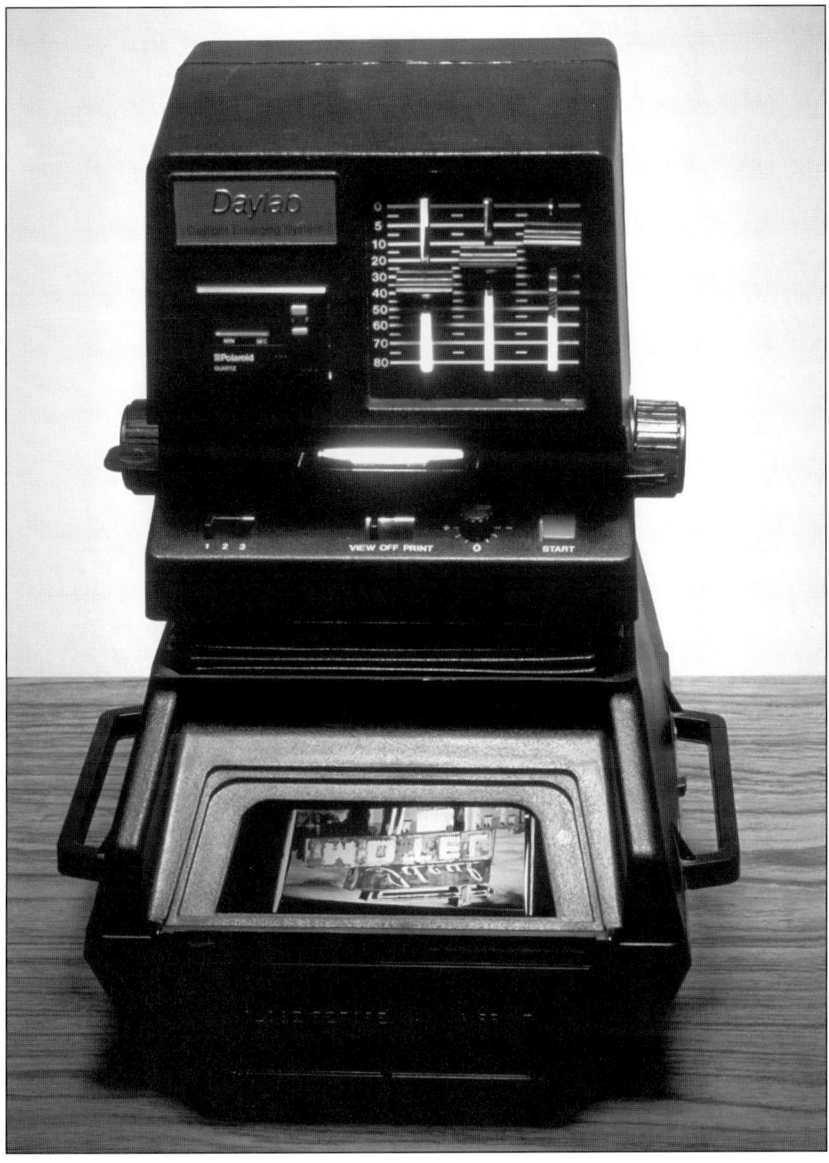

Fig. 10.4: *Because actual printing is carried out in a light-tight compartment, the DayLab machines may be used in normal room light. Be sure to reverse the image before printing.*

head featured on its predecessor, so minute adjustments are a snap. A built-in timer is in place for black and white or color films, but is not adjustable and will only time to full development. Since development needs to be timed to your preference, not Polaroid's, the timer is essentially useless for transfer work. Like its older brother, it also features an exposure control, variable over several f-stops *(fig. 10.5)*.

The Daylab Junior comes with an AC/DC adapter but does not have battery capability. Even with a poorly planned timer, it is still an excellent introductory printer.

Care must be taken to pull any Polaroid film straight out from the holder (parallel to the table top), in one easy motion. Failure to pull it straight may result in inadequate chemistry reaching all areas of the film. The same is true of film pulled across dirty rollers, which will produce blotchy areas of inconsistent color. Consequently, if you complete the transfer process, any flaws in the carrier sheet will also transfer. If you hesitate on the pull, or use uneven speed, some areas will receive too much chemistry and may look "hot." Fortunately, a quick inspection of the positive prior to discarding it will reveal most problems.

Fig. 10.5: *The built-in dichroic color head in the DayLab machines make small adjustments in color balance extremely easy.*

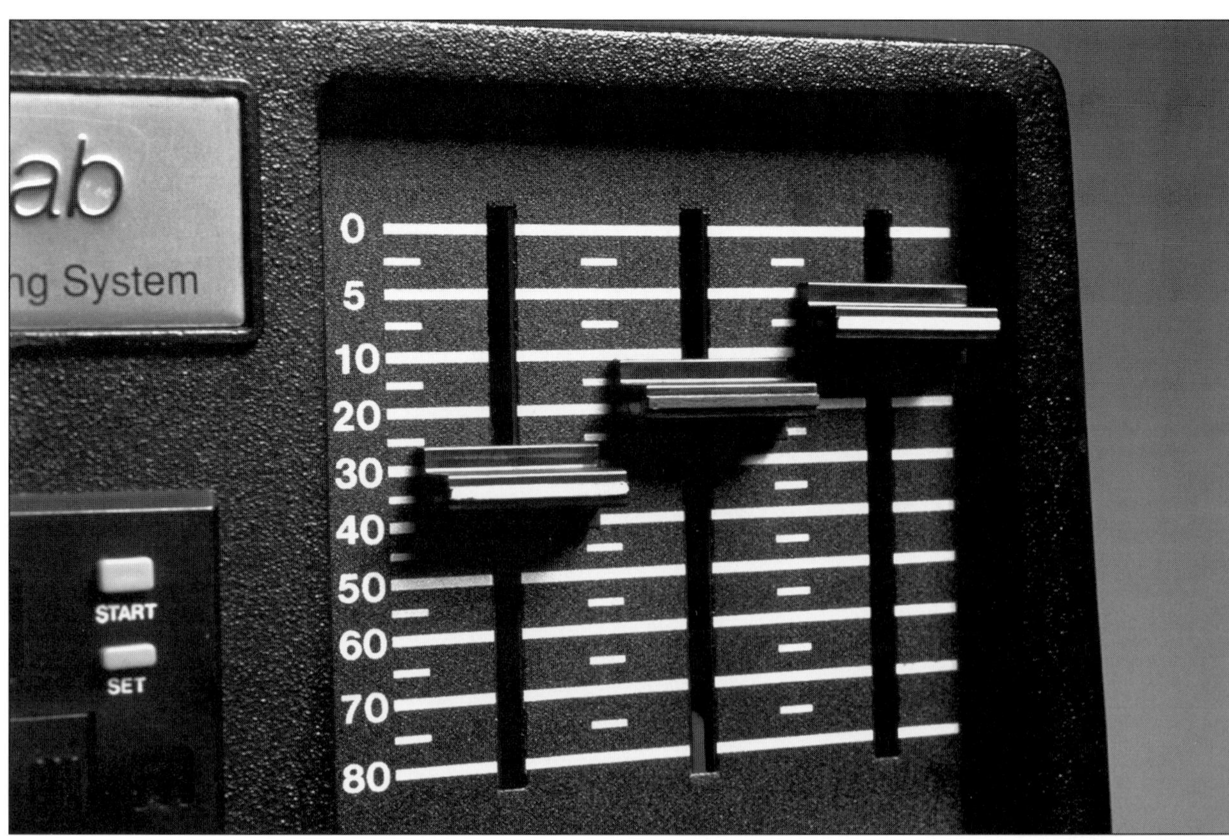

• PROJECTION PRINTING IN THE DARKROOM

If you're working in the darkroom, you can work from any size positive film original (up to the maximum your enlarger will handle, of course) and print directly onto Polaroid material. The size of your final enlargements is limited only by the focal length of your enlarger lens and the maximum size of the Polaroid material.

Polaroid Pack Size Films. For 108, 669, 679 or 689 film packs, you need a pack camera or other Polaroid pack back, such as those used with the Hasselblad® system, to act as a "processor." You can often find used pack cameras for as little as $2.00 at garage sales, thrift stores or flea markets.

First, cut a piece of white paper to the size of an exposed print and slide it into an empty Polaroid holder, against the pressure plate where the unexposed film used to be. Set a print easel or other right-angle form under the enlarger and brace that structure to hold the Polaroid holder in position under the enlarger *(fig. 10.6)*.

Project the transparency from the enlarger onto the white paper in the holder. Crop as you wish and using a color enlarging meter or the "Best Guess Method" (very popular), place the appropriate color correction filters under the lens or dial desired filtration into a color head. Set the f-stop and timer.

QUICK TIPS:

When projection printing an image for the first time it's always a good idea to expose a test and process it for the full cycle. This allows you to view a totally finished print and judge exposure and color before going through the additional time and expense of an actual transfer.

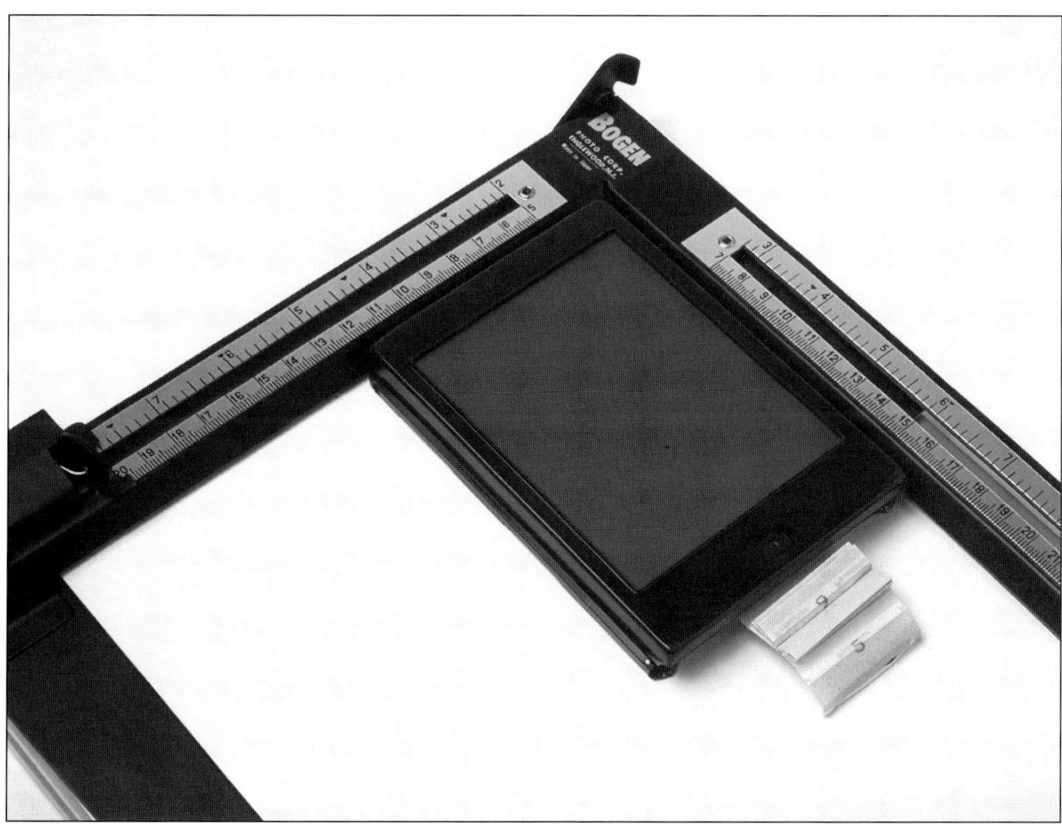

Fig. 10.6: *In the dark, you can always find the right place for the film pack if you place it in the corner of an ordinary easel.*

In order to make color corrections to projected Polaroid, you may use the following guidelines:

DESIRED RESULT	ADD (OR)	SUBTRACT
Less Yellow	Cyan + Magenta	Yellow
More Yellow	Yellow	Cyan + Magenta
Less Red	Cyan	Magenta + Yellow
More Red	Magenta + Yellow	Cyan
Less Magenta	Yellow + Cyan	Magenta
More Magenta	Magenta	Yellow + Cyan
Less Blue	Yellow	Cyan + Magenta
More Blue	Cyan + Magenta	Yellow
Less Cyan	Magenta + Yellow	Cyan
More Cyan	Cyan	Magenta + Yellow
Less Green	Magenta	Yellow + Cyan
More Green	Yellow + Cyan	Magenta

It's been my experience that Polaroid's publications regarding the transfer process and how it's used in the darkroom are based on equipment and voltages that would be "best case" field test situations (for them). My experiments would indicate most exposures should be reduced by at least two stops from the printed estimates (bear in mind that other equipment may produce different results) to achieve what I feel are optimum results. The transfer process is rich on the cyan and blue side because of how the dye layers transfer color to the receptor. Consequently, adding up to 20Y (20 points of yellow color correction – "20cc") plus 30M (30cc magenta) in addition to Polaroid's recommendations may produce much more pleasing overall tones, and much more accurate skin tones on your transfer. Your experience with your own originals will determine exposure and filtration packages that you like best with the film and paper you're comfortable using. Like any other film, Polaroid material varies from batch to batch, so I recommend that when you find some you like that you buy as much film from the same emulsion batch as you can afford, then store it until you need it. Follow the manufacturer's recommendations for storage and use it before its expiration date.

"Your experience ... will determine exposure and filtration packages that you like best ..."

When ready, remove the empty holder that you used for position and turn off all darkroom lights. If your timer has a separate safelight switch, make certain it's off as darkroom safelight will fog exposed, undeveloped film. In the dark, place the holder and unexposed film in the previously determined position against the easel. Make the exposure and, in the dark, return the pack to your "processor." When you're back in the light and ready to make a transfer, pull the film through the holder and begin processing.

Type 59, Type 79 (PolaColor Pro 100), and Type 64T. These envelopes incorporate both 4x5 negative and positive material and are used one sheet at a time, loaded, as needed, into a Polaroid Film Holder before exposure. This holder also acts as a processor for the exposed sheets.

Unlike the pack films, the 4x5 holder does not lie flat, and must be braced parallel to the film plane prior to setting the enlarger. The "brace" can be as simple as a film box of the correct height, and it's a good idea to build it around the film holder as well as under it. Tape it in place, so it won't move but can be easily found in the dark *(fig. 10.7)*.

Fig. 10.7: *This brace for the 4x5 Polaroid holder was simply made by taping two 50 sheet film boxes together, then taping the holder on the top. Any support will do, as long as the film plane is parallel to the enlarger.*

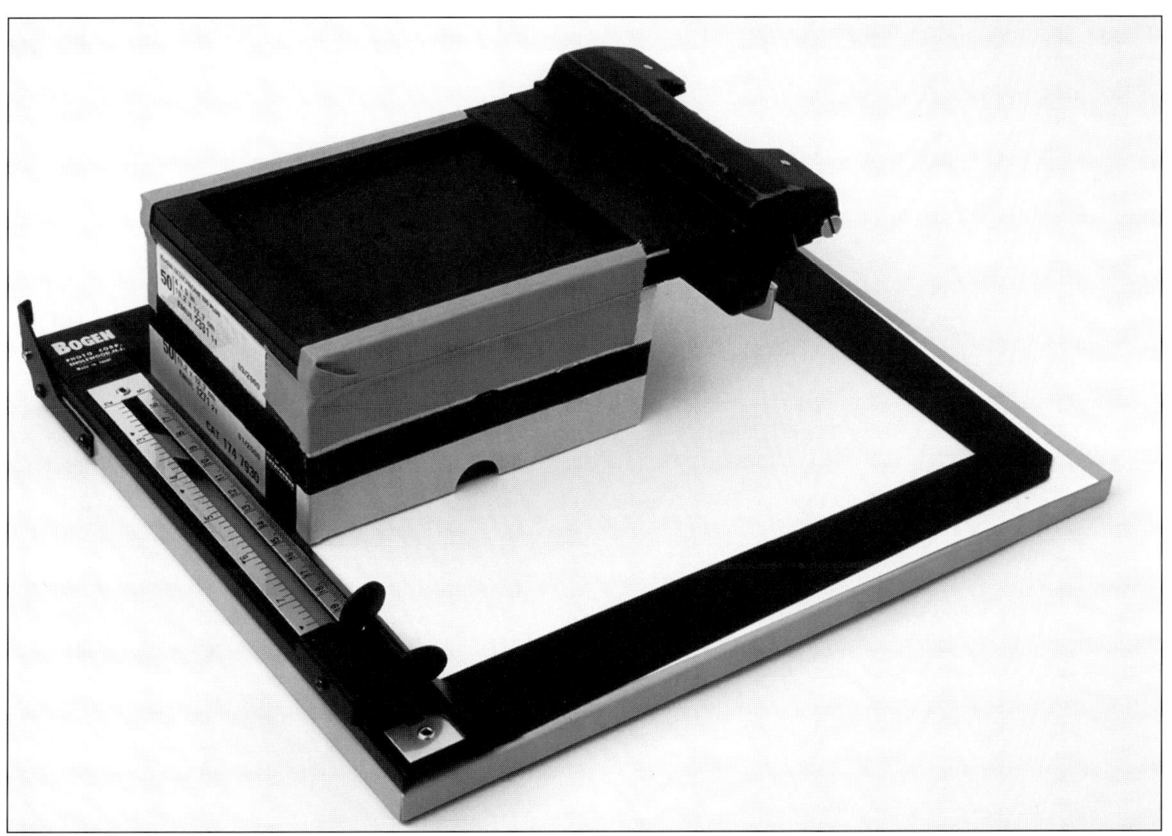

QUICK TIPS:

When projection printing onto any Polaroid material with an enlarger in the darkroom or with the DayLab, place the original transparency upside down (emulsion up) in the film carrier, otherwise your transferred result will be reversed. This is because you must expose the additional negative sheet before the true "positive to positive" effect is achieved. This is not necessary when using Vivitar or Polaroid units.

In order to pre-determine cropping and composition, it will be necessary to cut a piece of thick white paper or card stock to the overall dimensions of the Polaroid sheet. With this sheet in the holder and the holder in the brace, project the image from the enlarger onto the sheet, crop and adjust the enlarger as necessary and then remove the sheet before loading unexposed film.

After setting the enlarger, Types 59, 79 or 64T should be loaded in room light. Move the lever to the "load" position and insert the film sheet. The film envelope must be loaded with the correct side ("this side toward lens") facing out, or you will project onto the opaque side of the film. When loaded, turn off the room lights, pull the tab gently until it stops, and place the holder in the brace. Make the exposure and return the film to the envelope. When you're back in the light and ready to make a transfer, pull the film through the holder and begin processing. Be certain you understand the operation of the holder, especially the "load" and "unload" functions of the lever. 4x5 film is expensive, and you sometimes make mistakes even when you do everything else correctly.

All other steps will be the same.

Type 809. For the 8x10 material, you also need a separate processor for the film. Calumet makes a hand-crank processor that works just fine and which is not as expensive as Polaroid's motorized version. You must have one or the other to burst and spread the chemical pouch evenly and consistently. (Check your local professional Polaroid dealers, many have units to rent.)

A Polaroid 8x10 film holder is included with the processor, and that's what you'll use to position the film under the enlarger before and during exposure.

Be certain you understand the operation of the processor before you start. For 809 images, the negative and positive are separate pieces, safe to handle in room light, joined together for the first time in the processor. They must be loaded correctly or the film will be wasted. Type 809, per sheet, is three times the cost of Type 59, so read and understand the instructions.

All other steps will be the same.

• A UNIQUE TRICK FOR PROJECTION PRINTING

Greg Halvorson, a professional photographic equipment dealer, offers this low-tech but fabulous trick that will work under any enlarger.

To render a painterly, somewhat abstract, look to your final image, take a piece of clean glass and smear petroleum jelly onto the top surface. Using your fingers, rub a pattern across the glass. Don't try to smooth it out, you want to make textures with your fingers (after one exposure you'll understand this completely, so let your fingers go wherever they feel like going for the first one. You'll develop your own style shortly).

When finished, and when ready for the projection exposure, lay the jellied glass over the unexposed film, jelly side up, then hit the exposure button and expose the Polaroid film. Exposure will be short, even at a small aperture such as f-22, and since depth of field is extended at small apertures, the exposure through the jellied glass will produce sharp shadows from the smear lines. These in turn will bend or shade the light. (Minor exposure adjustment may be necessary to compensate for the additional density of the glass.) The end result is a beautiful, almost Impressionistic effect *(fig. 10.1)*.

This will also work with the Daylab II Slide Printer. Just cut a piece of glass larger than the film window in your selected module and rub petroleum jelly onto that before making any exposure.

"... exposure through the jellied glass will produce sharp shadows from the smear lines."

• LIVE TRANSFERS

Live transfers are difficult. Made with a camera that either accepts or was made only for Polaroid film, the taken photograph is imbibed, separated and transferred on the spot, one-at-a-time. Unless you shoot something that doesn't move, corrections between exposures are difficult *(fig. 10.2)*.

In the 1960's Polaroid produced a new series of amateur cameras designed to replace the old, split-roll color cameras with a new "pack" that held both positive and negative material in one holder and did not require threading through rollers. These cameras, beginning with the basic Model 100, were once tremendously popular because of their ease of use and quality of image, and are now quite desirable as transfer tools.

Although discontinued for many years, pack cameras are readily available at very affordable prices through garage sales and camera swaps *(fig. 10.8)*. Even the most basic Model 100 makes fine live transfers, but should you be lucky enough to find the Model 880, which features a glass

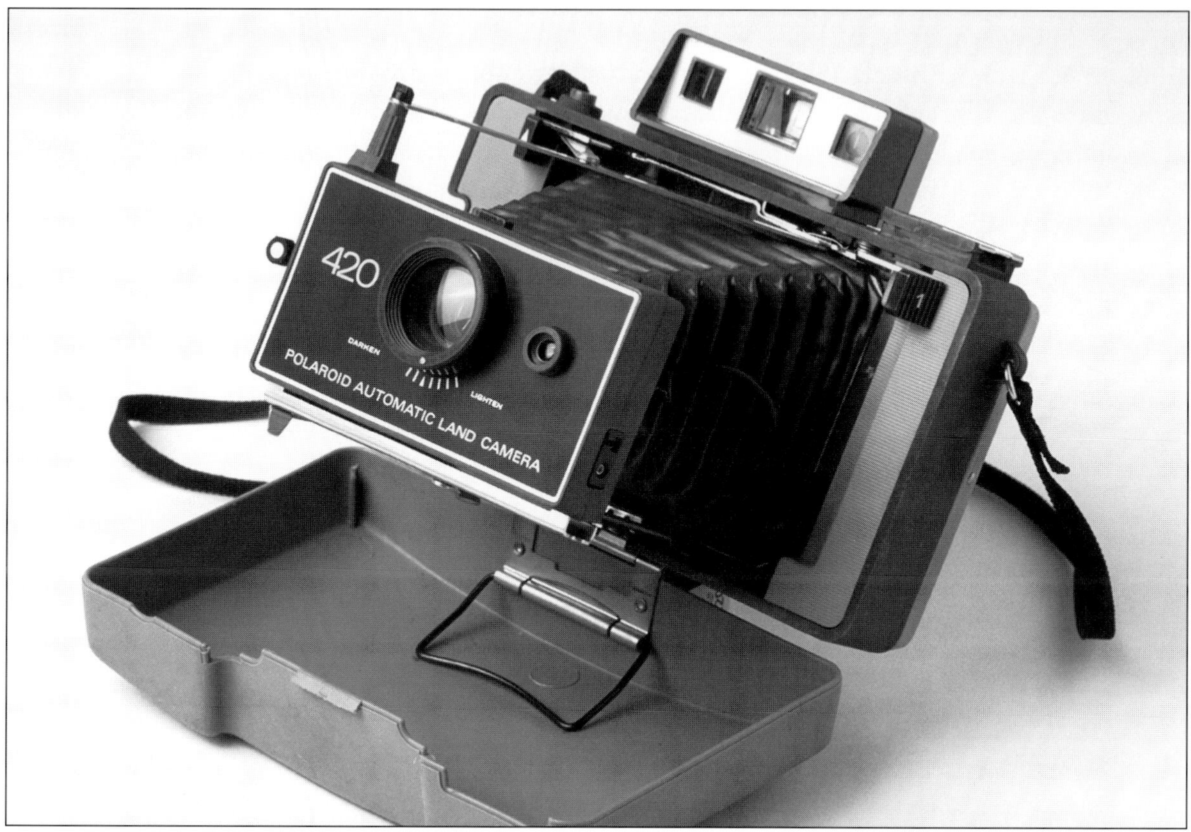

Fig. 10.8: *The Polaroid model 420, which still works perfectly, was purchased at a garage sale for $2.00. This model also features a built-in development timer on the back.*

lens, multi-speed shutter and adjustable iris, buy it immediately (as a friend of mine recently did, finding his in a second hand store for $10.00). Even if it doesn't work, they are relatively easy to have fixed, and worth every penny.

Like all photographic manufacturers, Polaroid has endorsed, created and subsequently withdrawn, many useful pieces of gear. These may still be found in used camera bins, on the Internet, in camera swap meets or even at garage or charity sales. Here is a descriptive list of the most worthwhile equipment.

The Polaroid 600 SE. Even better for live transfers than the basic pack machine, this dedicated Polaroid camera features interchangeable Mamiya® optics for crystal clear prints. A deluxe pistol grip and a wide, center-weighted base make this unit easy to hand hold even at very slow shutter speeds (I've had better than average success at one second).

This is what the 880 aspired to be, and is without a doubt the best "live transfer" camera money can buy.

Unfortunately, it was recently back-burnered by Polaroid and its future is uncertain.

The Vivitar® Instant Slide Printer. This wonderful self-contained machine allows direct copies from 35mm slides to Polaroid 3 $^{1}/_{4}$ x 4 $^{1}/_{4}$ color material without a darkroom. It works off AA batteries, with an AC adapter available. The adapter is recommended if you plan on making a lot of copies. This machine also makes terrific black and

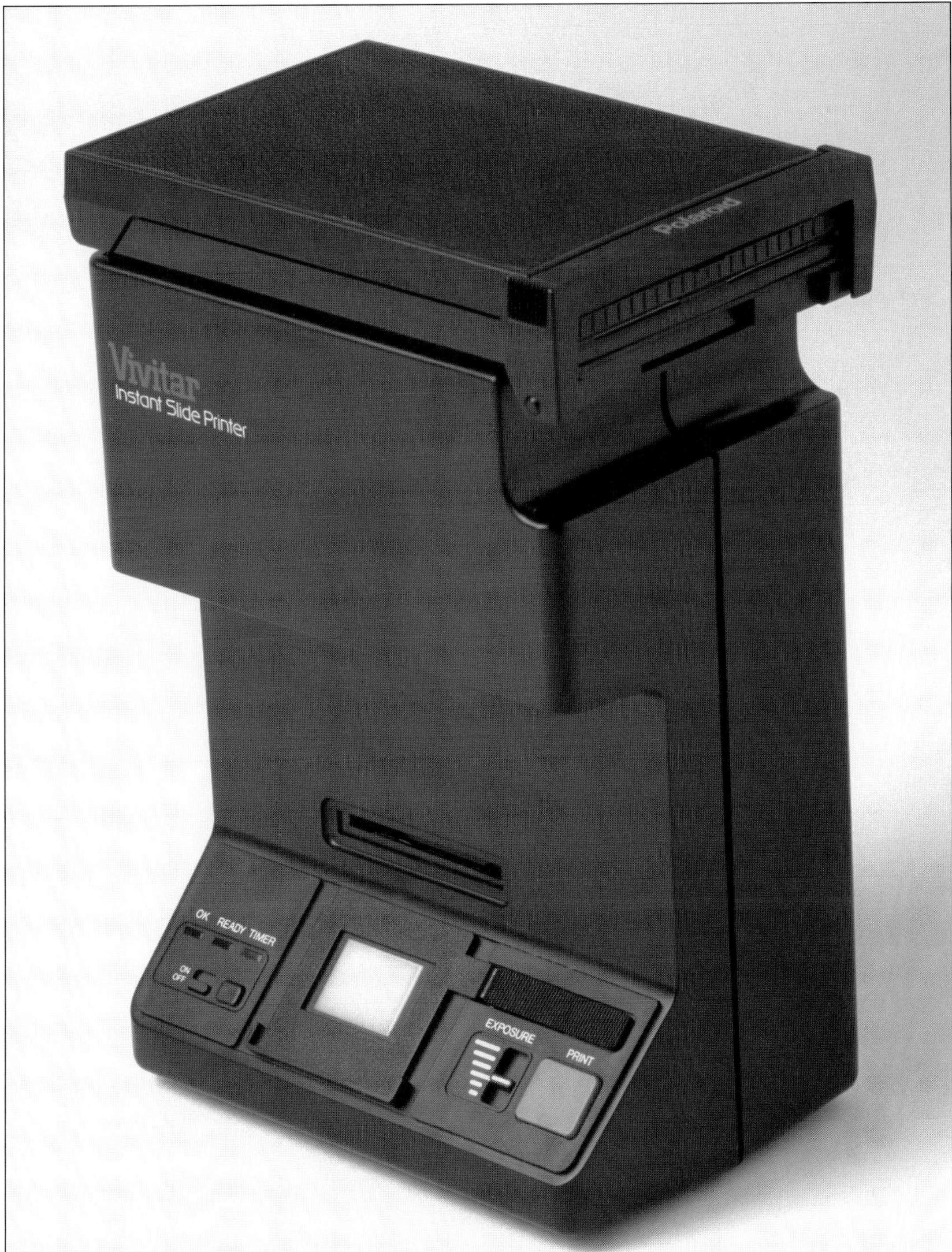

Fig. 10.9: *The Vivitar Polaroid slide printer.*

white Polaroid prints from color slides, as well as full color prints when fully developed but not transferred *(fig. 10.9)*.

When you're ready to copy an image, place the slide you're working with onto the small backlit screen on the front. Notice that the screen shows image area smaller than the slide itself. 35mm slides do not crop naturally to Polaroid proportions, so some cropping is necessary. Moving the slide shelf back and forth shows you what cropping options you have; as you move the slide, you also move the carrier inside the machine, so what you see is pretty much what you'll get. You may also flip the slide upside down, or flop it right to left, as that may change the perception of the image just enough to make your final crop more interesting.

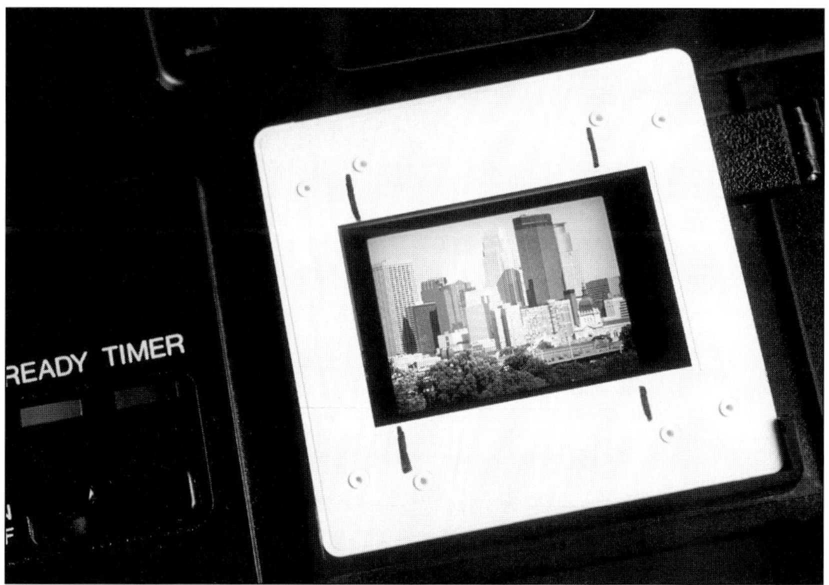

Fig. 10.10: *Marking crops on the slide mount will make it easier to repeat prints made with the Vivitar.*

QUICK TIPS:

Multiple exposures with varying exposures are always difficult to produce. Such images require precise control during exposure. To make it easier to duplicate them or to build on previous efforts, simply mark the exposure control lever on the Vivitar machine from one to six, noting on the backs of a sample print which image was exposed in what order and at what number.

An additional aid might be to mark final crops on the slide mount prior to placing it in the machine, in order to repeat compositions more easily *(fig. 10. 10)*.

When you're happy with the crop, place the slide (the same way as you viewed it on the screen) into the receptacle just above the viewer.

When the exposure is made, a built-in automatic strobe reads the density of the original and exposes the film to an attached holder on top of the unit. Exposure may be adjusted in half-stop increments.

Because of its small size and affordable low price, this unit provides a terrific way to begin exploration the Polaroid Transfer process. Even though it's been discontinued, I've seen many of them at used equipment outlets. If you're lucky enough to find an AC adapter for the unit, be certain to buy it as well.

The 8x10 Polaroid Printer. Another self contained unit, this machine is capable of enlarging 35mm slides to

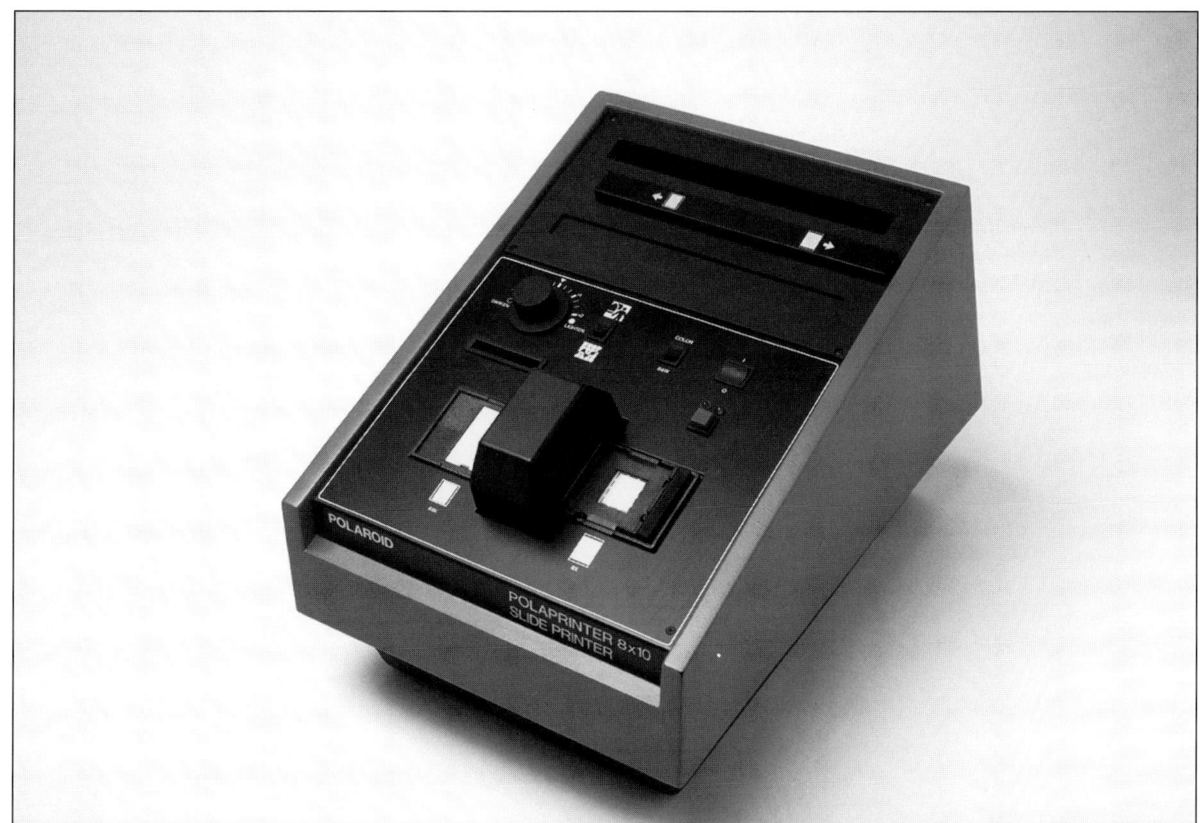

Fig. 10.11: *The 8x11 Polaroid Printer.*

8x10 size. It features either a full image mode, in which the entire 35mm area is projected, or a tighter crop which fully fills the 8x10 area. Exposure is adjustable in 1/3 stop increments with additional controls for black and white or color originals. A color filter holder is also included and, as with the Vivitar unit, exposure is automatic through the strobe sensor.

Most exposures will be made with the machine set for "normal," and, unfortunately, there is no way short of trying a sheet of film to know if that will be correct for your tastes.

Although it's no longer made, it's still a great tool. If you find one for rental, give it a try. If you can find a used one at an affordable price, snap it up *(fig. 10.11)*.

QUICK TIPS:

The Rosco Company makes colored filter gels for theatrical and studio lights. They package a sample swatch of each color they sell (well over 100) into a small, rivet bound booklet, available free at any Rosco outlet (Professional camera stores, theatrical or performance supply houses, professional motion picture supply houses). They may easily be trimmed to a 2" length without removing them from the booklet and will fit perfectly into either the Vivitar or Polaroid slide printer units. Each color is represented in a variety of densities so you can make slight or extreme filtration selections with ease.

Chapter 11

CARE AND KEEPING OF FINAL IMAGES

"... transfers seem to age and fade evenly."

A traditional color print should last at least twenty years before showing any signs of age. Image fading or color shifting is inevitable, but is accelerated by exposure to strong, direct sunlight or bright fluorescents. Polaroid prints are no exception – many Type 108 prints made when the film was introduced in the '60s and stored over the years in albums or boxes are just as brilliant now as when they were made.

Unfortunately, Polaroid image transfers do not share the same longevity. I suspect it simply may be because the image chemistry is diluted by the process itself. Transfers seem to be more sensitive to light. Images of mine that have received indirect yet strong sunlight, without benefit of ultraviolet glass or other UV protection, show some fading after five years. Yet, if one carefully stores original transfers in archival albums or other protected places, they appear to have the same life as a conventional print.

This color instability of a Polaroid transfer may actually be something of an asset. While traditional C-prints usually color shift to magenta as they get older, transfers seem to age and fade evenly. Periodic copying or scanning of these images as they lose brilliance and contrast will give you variations to work with later.

Because each Polaroid transfer is a unique original, many artists require tested methods of reproduction in order to offer duplicates of their finest work. Whether you do the copy work or farm it out to a service bureau, here are some options you should consider.

The obvious first method is to copy the transfer using two copy lights set at the traditional 45° angle to the print *(fig. 11.1)*.

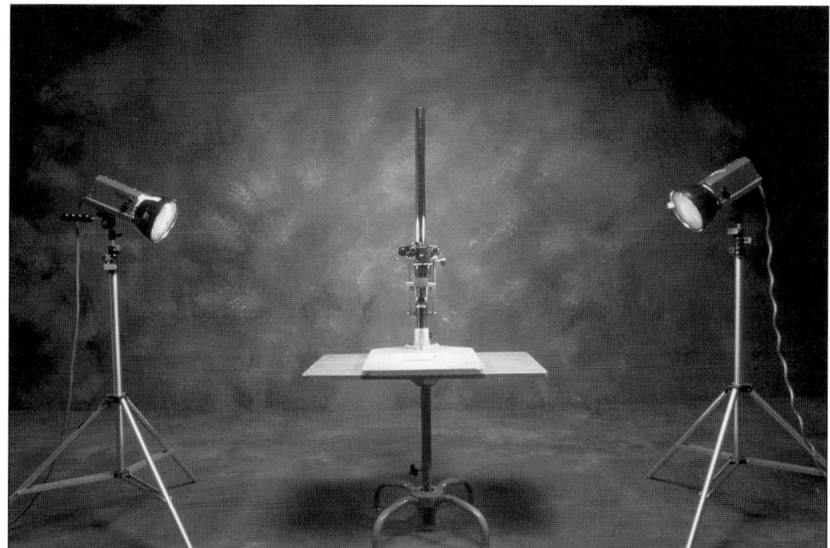

Fig. 11.1: *A typical, approximately 45 degree, two-light copy setup.*

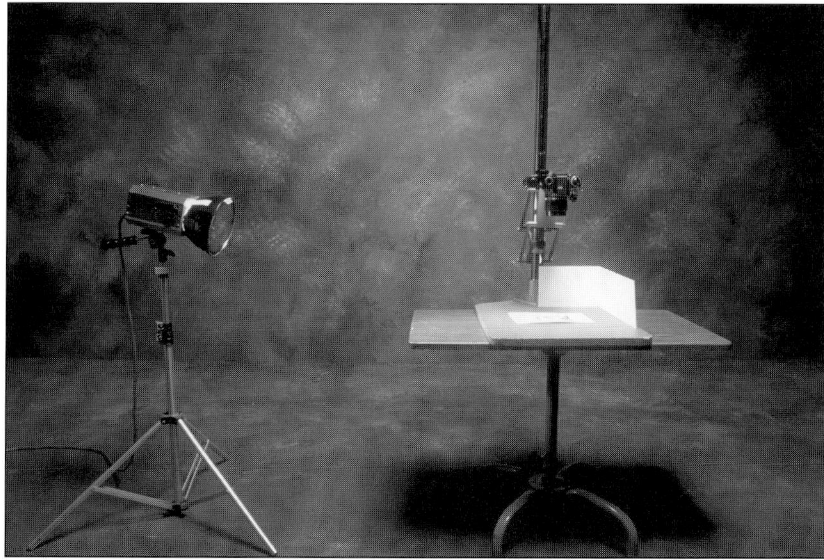

Fig. 11.2: *Using one light at approximately 30 degrees will dramatically enhance the textures of Polaroid transfers.*

This is perfectly acceptable and will result in excellent copies on color or black and white material.

Since Polaroids have such a personal look to them, try lighting with only one copy light, set to approximately 30°. Now the light skims, more than floods, the picture. If the transferred picture shows a strong source light, set the copy light to mimic the angle of the source light, so that the shadows thrown by the paper texture follow those in the image itself. If you find the texture shadows from the copy light to be too intense, you can knock them back by setting up a white card on the opposite side, several inches from the border, to kick some light back into the shadows. Don't get rid of too much shadow – the idea is to accent the texture of the receptor paper *(fig. 11.2)*.

"C-print paper and color negative film get better and more stable every day..."

If you copy to color negative film, you can have traditional negative-to-paper color prints, called "C-prints," made in almost any size. The larger the copy negative, the bigger the potential final print. Generally, a 4"x5" color copy negative is more than adequate for most applications. C-print paper and color negative film get better and more stable every day, and such prints are the least expensive of all the color print processes. Negatives may also be scanned to digital files. When sending the file to a service provider for output, a good color-correct print should accompany the file to guarantee correct final color.

The most versatile copy film is the color transparency. It's the easiest to judge for color balance and density when backlit by a color-corrected light box. It's also the film of choice for digital scans and traditional color separations for printing. One may produce color or black and white internegatives for prints or produce positive to paper prints, called "R-prints". Ilfochromes (formerly Cibachromes), probably the most archivally stable, color saturated prints around, can also be made directly from the original transparency.

For an unexpected, artistic look you might consider copying directly to black and white film and printing onto the very high quality black and white fine art papers currently available. If you're darkroom savvy, you can make the prints yourself or send them out to a custom printer.

An extremely effective way of creating simple duplicates of your transfers is to have them copied on a state-of-the-art color copier. Be certain to check, with the manufacturer if necessary, as to the archival qualities of the ink and paper the copier uses. Some copies last considerably longer than others but none will last as long as a C-print. If possible, substitute better/more interesting paper for the normal copy paper. It's worth the money to test any image before running a large batch of copies.

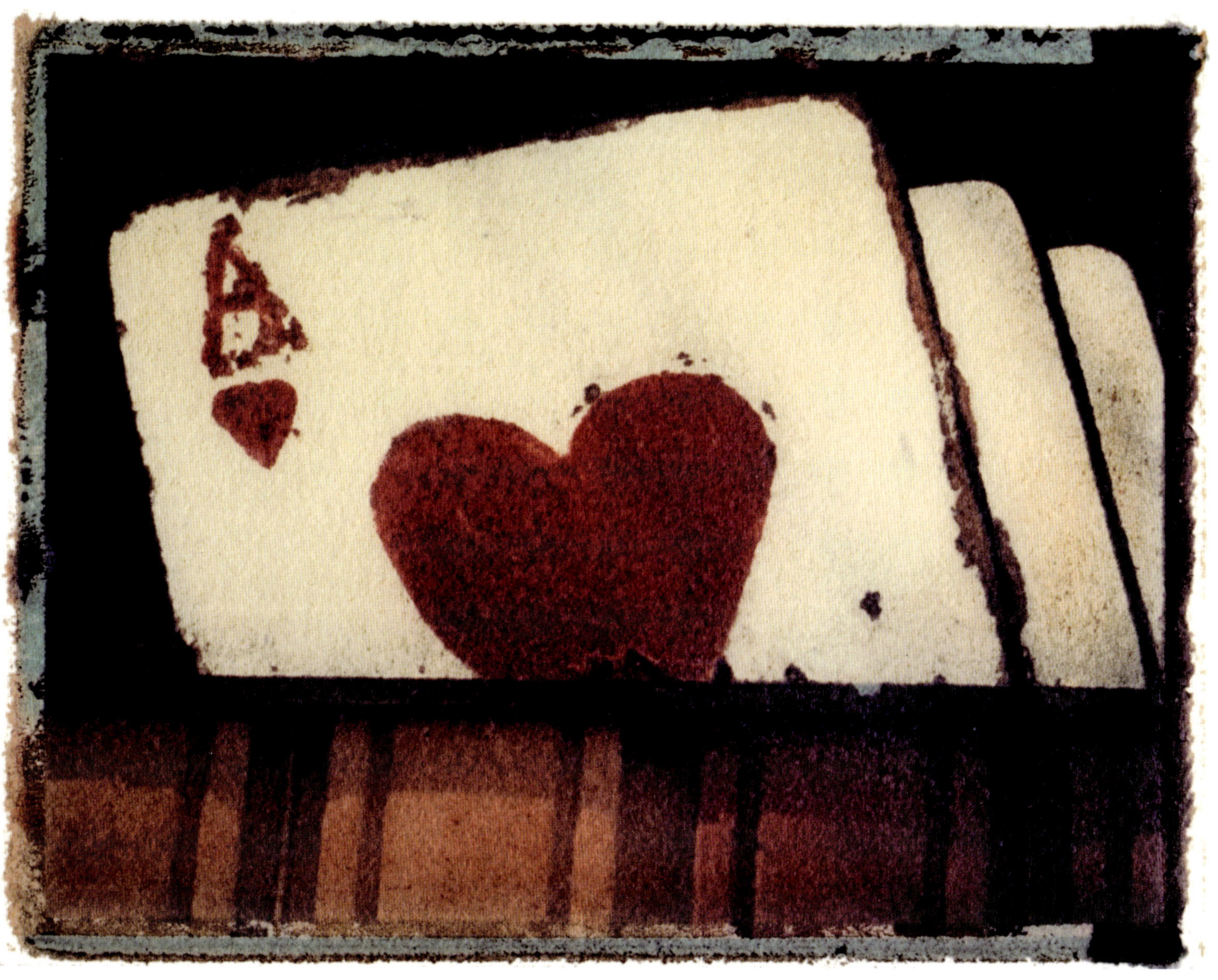

Fig. 12.1: *The original 35mm slide was taken into Photoshop where the whites were brightened and the contrast increased. The digital file was then burned as a new slide and transferred. Type 669, Arches paper.*

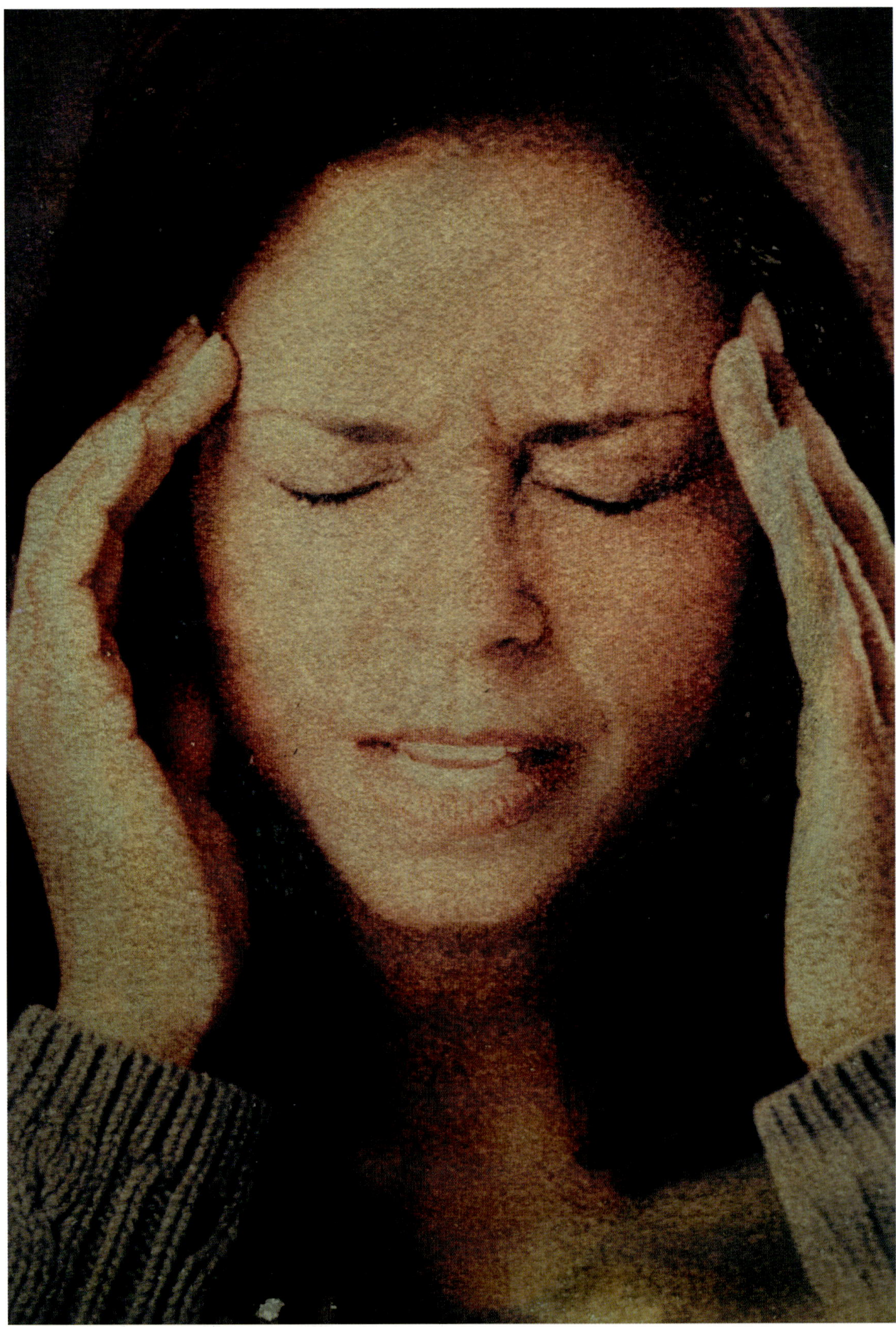

Fig. 12.2: *Polaroid transfers lend themselves to many commercial and editorial uses. The texture of the transfer was enhanced by lightly wiping the wet transfer with a damp paper towel, using a circular motion.*

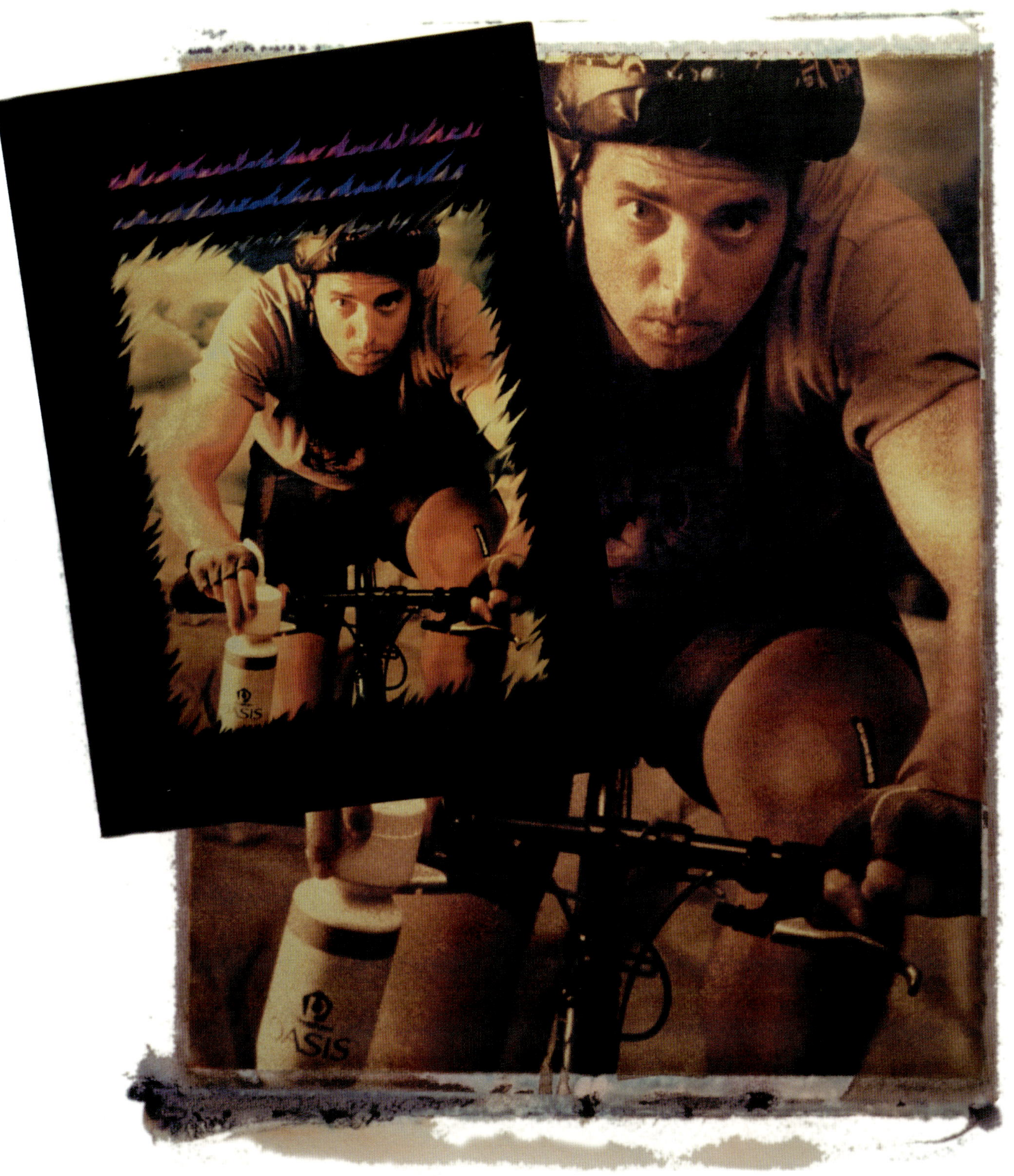

Fig. 12.3: *An example of an 8x10 polaroid transfer and the final, printed advertising piece.*

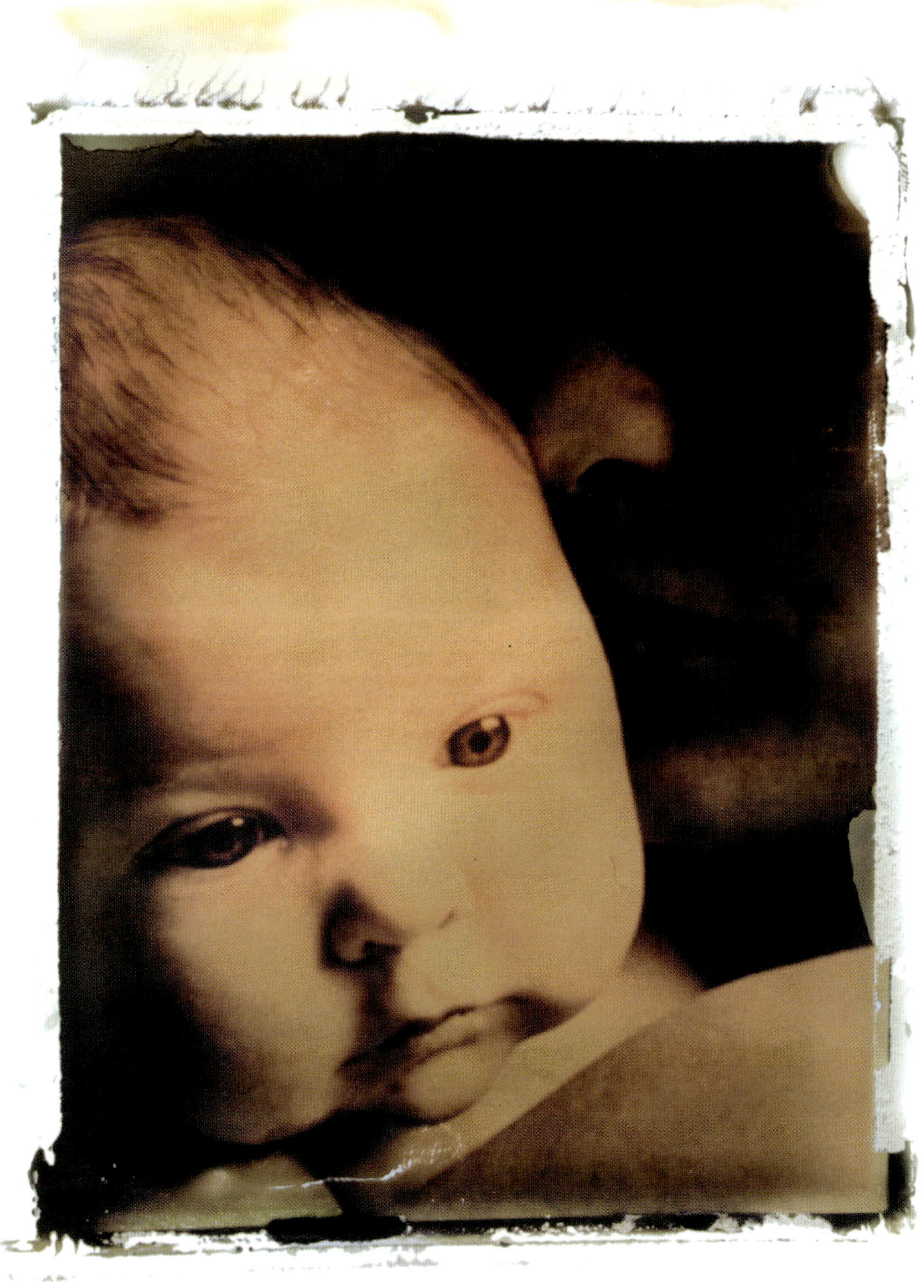

Fig. 12.4: *Color copy slide of a black and white print transferred to Epson Ink Jet Paper. Type 669.*

Chapter 12
What's New, What's Next

Digital Technology

Recent developments in digital equipment and their subsequent (and continuing) reductions in price have made it possible to do more with Polaroid images than ever before. Serious fans of digital imaging have invested in their own computer work stations, but others can easily learn about and rent time on necessary equipment at local digital service centers or cutting-edge printing shops.

"Recent developments in digital equipment ... have made it possible to do more with Polaroid images than ever before."

Unfortunately, there is almost no room in this book for any instruction in programs such as Photoshop® or Live Picture®. For the next few paragraphs, let's assume you are reasonably proficient with image-editing software, and that you have either scanned Polaroid images yourself, using a flatbed or drum scanner, or that you have copied your images and had them placed on a Kodak PhotoCD or other such product. Bear in mind that if you use a flatbed or drum scanner to scan originals, you cannot control the texture shadows as you can with a copy light.

We'll also assume that you have used your image transfer and digital scan, along with your image editing software, and created a modern masterpiece. You have many options for reproduction.

Although the Iris® was one of the first inkjet printers used for fine art, many more have entered the market, coining a new, generic name for such a print: Giclée. My guess is the name, pronounced "zhee-clay," was coined when an art gallery director, looking at the beautiful new works, decided no one would buy them if they were called "computer driven micro-inkjet prints." Coined in France, the word "Giclée" seemed appropriate, as it means "to squirt" (readers may draw their own conclusions as to the actual hedonistic spin the French infer with the word). Prints from these machines can be made on regular matte or glossy paper, watercolor paper or canvas. Many machines use rolled stock at least 36" wide, so prints can be quite large at reasonable prices *(fig. 12.5)*.

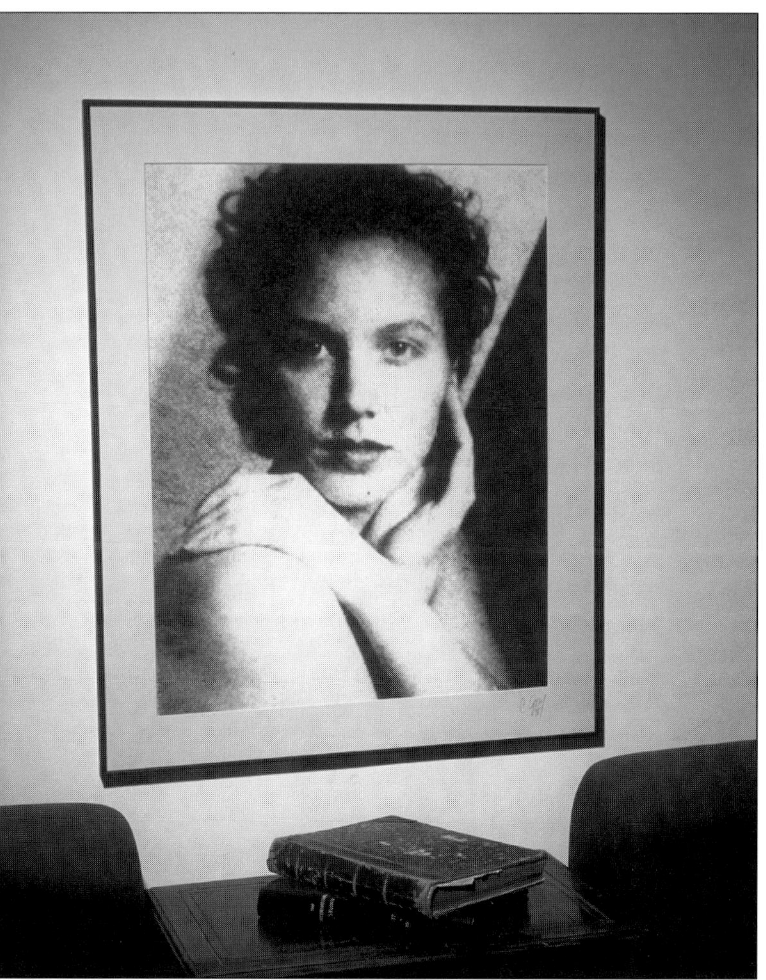

Fig. 12.5: *End result of the 7-Step Print-to-Print process. This Giclée print, measuring 24"x34" and printed on canvas, originated from a pack size Pro 100 transfer made with the hot iron process.*

QUICK TIPS:

Seven steps from black and white transfer to Giclée, using easy to find digital equipment:

1. Make black and white print
2. Copy onto color slide material
3. Polaroid transfer to appropriate receptor
4. Copy transfer to color slide, or scan to digital file
5. Scan to Kodak PhotoCD, or save file on computer
6. Photoshop for any necessary retouching or alterations
7. Output through Giclée printer

A number of manufacturers, such as Epson, have introduced small inkjet printers that produce near-photographic quality prints on a number of flat and textured paper surfaces. Although the archival properties of these prints is still questionable, they can be used as new "masters" for a variety of applications:

Scan transfers and lift-offs and digitally enhance as desired. Make inkjet prints and copy those to large format negatives or transparencies which are then used to produce "C" or "R" prints for display or sale.

Make inkjet prints and copy onto 35mm color or black and white slide film. Make new transfers from these manipulated images *(fig. 12.1)*.

Polaroid also makes a Film Recorder device. While this machine is admittedly expensive, it allows you to print digital image files directly to Polaroid film. This is about the cleanest Polaroid image one can make and also allows for the most easily modified transfer.

POLAROID NEGATIVE

Interesting effects can also be obtained by copying Polaroid color negatives, either from spent, transferred film or from completely developed images as would be left over after an emulsion lift-off. Try using polarized light to intensify any remaining color. For best results, place a polarizing filter over the source light as well as the camera lens, and bracket the exposures onto color slide film so they are usable as new originals for transfers. For cleaner color, soak any dried negatives in water for a few minutes before copying.

"Try using polarized light to intensify any remaining color."

If you desire reproductions, such copies may be made by traditional analog methods or brought into a digital system, enhanced and output to new film by methods previously discussed.

Color negatives may be used, either copy negatives of a positive you're using or unrelated images, to produce reversed tones around, behind or through the positive. Interesting effects can also be obtained by contact printing a positive to black and white material and then sandwiching the two together, slightly out of register.

The number of photographic techniques and methods that may be used with Polaroid material is virtually unlimited. In fact, if there are any limitations at all, they're found only in your imagination. As mentioned previously, anything you feel like trying is worth at least one sheet of film. Within the sum total of those individual sheets may be found the essence of your personal style.

Chapter 13

FINDING MARKETS FOR YOUR WORK

"Professional photographers are frequently utilized as problem solvers ..."

Like so many other techniques, Polaroid transfer should be in every photographer's repertoire and visible in their portfolios. Professional photographers are frequently utilized as problem solvers because they can interpret an abstract concept and translate it to a two-dimensional piece of paper. This available bag of tricks every photographer carries, and its relative depth, often determines the degree of success a photographer can bring to a commercial project.

EDITORIAL MARKETS

Like every market, editorial users are constantly looking for new treatments to spice up otherwise dull visual reportage. There are limits to the number of ways a portrait of an executive or other subject can be spiffed up in any given publication, even when an art director is a Photoshop wizard. Photographers who have a command of Polaroid transfer techniques may have a leg up on those who don't, as editors may wish to cash in on their knowledge. In editorial photography, images are frequently used as set pieces for stories, and transfers are useful to establish those moods or tones. Transfers, when used as large illustrations behind or with a particular story, can be especially effective as a visual device. Periodicals with a more up-tempo look may use Polaroid transfers even more regularly, although they may digitally alter your images even further. Editors accustomed to working with digital files (as more and more are) will appreciate well done manipulations *(fig 12.2)*.

ADVERTISING/COMMERCIAL PHOTOGRAPHY

If it is true that "art is the medium of the masses," as the late actor and art collector Vincent Price once said, then advertising is the vehicle which propels that art. An insatiable seeker and consumer of technique, the advertising industry made overnight stars of many photographers who were in control of a particular technique. If you are a professional photographer involved with advertising, it may be to your advantage to devote a portion of your portfolio to your best transfers. Stretch yourself. Art directors and advertisers alike respond to images that grab attention *(fig. 12.3)*.

"... the advertising industry made overnight stars of many photographers ..."

There is a photographer I know who, upon getting the list of winners for the local advertising show, made each winner a personalized Polaroid transfer greeting card of congratulations. The expense for the project was high, and the amount of work enormous, but the payoff for this showcase of his work was equally spectacular. Seeing a high level of creativity, art directors called for portfolio reviews, as did editors and other photography users. A number of high profile jobs were offered for bid and some were won as a result of that promotion. Actual artistic satisfaction came with having the signed photos displayed on bulletin boards and cubicle walls for many months afterward.

COMMERCIAL AND PERSONAL PORTRAITURE

Photographers in portraiture field should consider Polaroid imagery as a starting point to more interesting pictures and higher invoices. Create a number of samples using transfers as a digital basis. Make giclée prints and place them in strategic locations around the studio, to be discovered as customers walk through. Answer questions as they arise and suggest the technique to your customers for their own photographs. Or, make a finished print and show it almost as an afterthought when the rest of the order is being picked up. I have seen both techniques used quite successfully *(fig. 12.4)*.

Another possibility for portrait use might be to copy old photographs and convert the copies to transfers, then to enhanced digital files *(fig. 13.1)*. Easily artsy, the Giclée versions are warmer and more interesting than traditional photographic copies. The extra money also looks better on your bottom line.

No matter how you work it, Polaroid images are exciting alternatives to traditional portraiture, made even more so by your great original image.

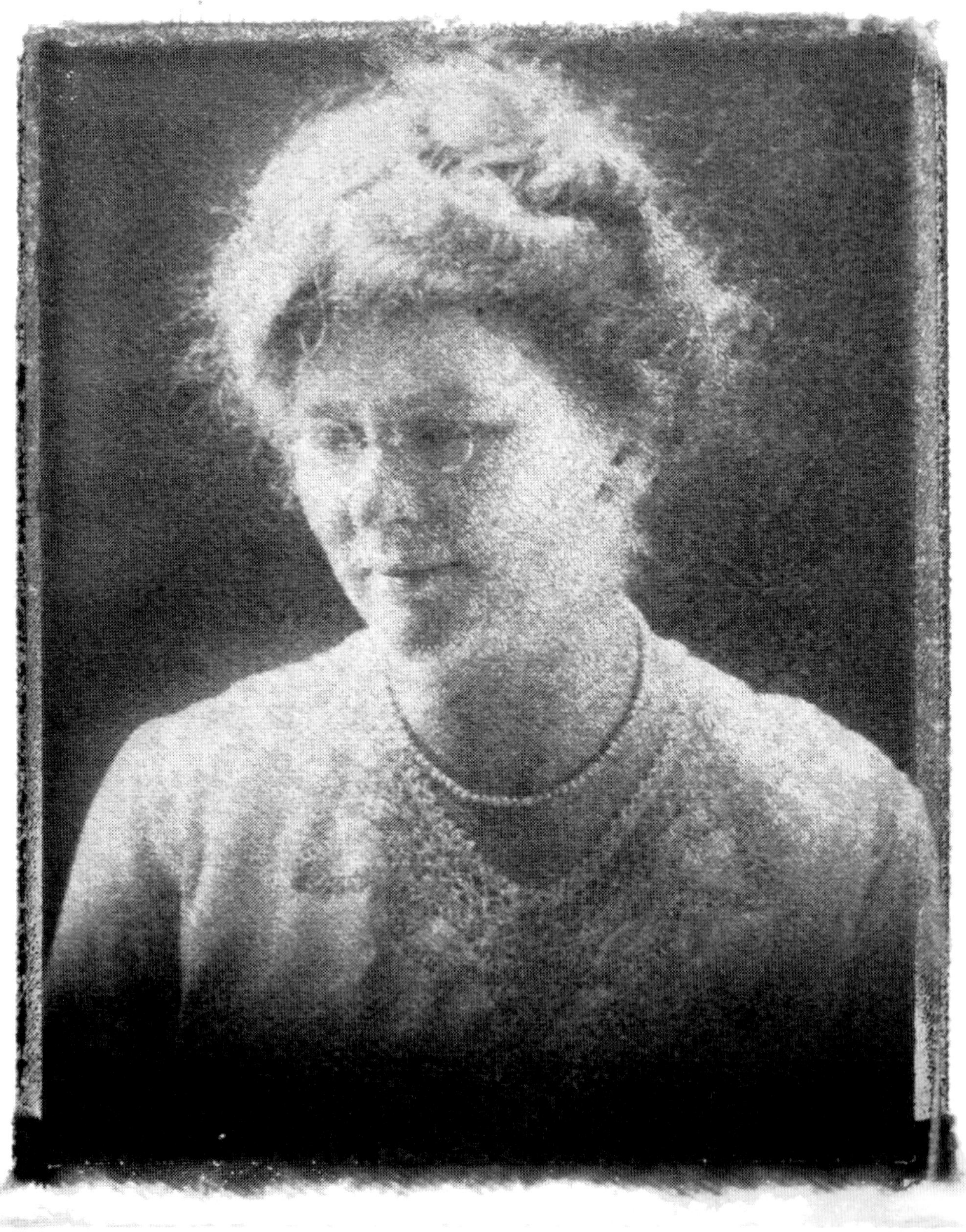

Fig. 13.1: *Making transfers from color slide copies of old photographs is an easy way to increase the artistic value of old images.*

Weddings or other Family Events

Considering the relentless competition within the wedding photography business, anything you can do to set your work above that of others counts as a significant coup. Exhibiting transfer and lift-off techniques, either on your sample wall or as speculation prints shown when your customer's order is placed or picked up, might contribute to the word of mouth advertising that's so crucial to continued success.

Fine Art

There are no limits to the approaches one might take to fine art when Polaroid transfers and/or lift-offs are included in the creative cycle.

One avenue is the art gallery. Commercial or underground, most larger cities publish a gallery guide which showcases a number of galleries along with their artists. Page through almost any of them and you will find at least one example of Polaroid transfer. Subject matter is varied, depending on artist, gallery specialty or area of the country, as you might guess. If you believe your work should be seen in art galleries, you are well advised to investigate any gallery thoroughly before sending any unsolicited material.

A word of caution regarding galleries: many gallery curators are not photographically literate but expect you to be. You must be ready to explain everything they'll need to understand to sell your work, should they choose to do so. Curators only desire to represent the highest caliber of work – should you acquire gallery representation, you should consider yourself both lucky and talented.

Fine art photographic treatments are not limited to art galleries – there are many commercial venues for such work, such as:

• **CD Covers**. Music CD covers are still works of art, although not as impressive as their original, 12x12 vinyl album counterparts. Still, many musicians, great and small, use renditions of Polaroid transfer images to illustrate their performances. If there's one thing to be said for album art, it's that there's always room for a new approach (the money is good, too).

• **Greeting Cards.** Many greeting card publishers appreciate Polaroid imagery for what it is and devote a portion of their annual catalogs to such pictures. A wise artist spends time looking at publisher's lines and deciding the

Quick Tips:

As a guest of a friend at his wedding, I had the opportunity to watch the photographers work. Two young shooters, lights and equipment in tow, photographed along with the "main" photographer. Everything they did was shot on Polaroid 4x5 Type 59, but nothing was processed on the spot. They explained their entire wedding photography business was based on Polaroid transfer, and that at some point within the next week they would process each piece of film, transfer it as a "one-shot" image, and, if it made the cut, bind it into a very unique album. They also explained that they were in high demand, as many couples thought such a product truly symbolized a personal, one-of-a-kind relationship.

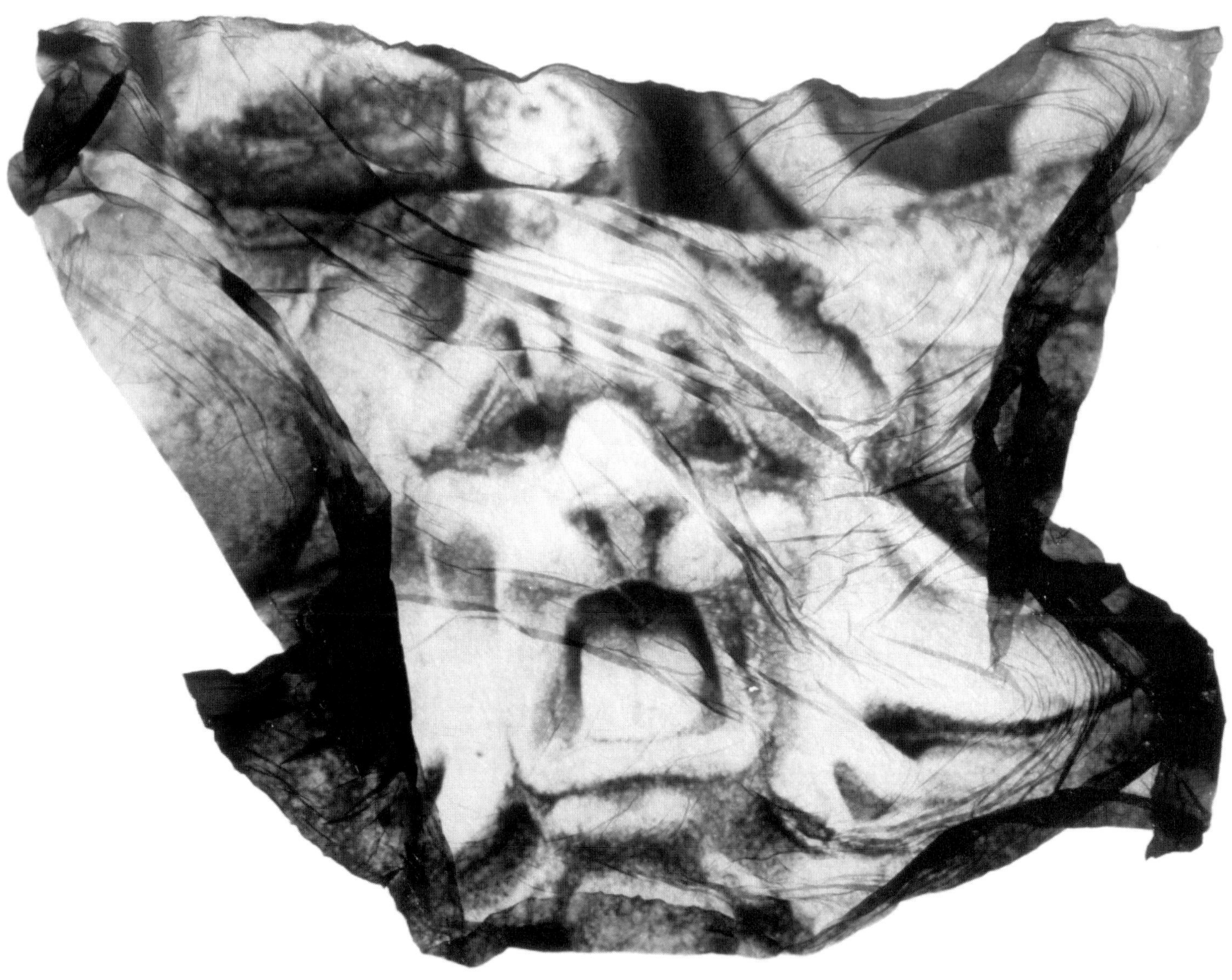

fig. 13.2: *Slight overexposure of the copy film made the overlaps of this lift-off even more interesting. Type 669, Arches paper.*

relevance of his or her work to a particular publisher before pursuing the issue any further.

If you're the type to showcase images at neighborhood or citywide art fairs and shows, you might consider home-made greeting cards made by cutting cover weight paper stock down to 7x10 and then scoring and folding to 5x7. Use color copies of your favorite Polaroid images on the covers and package with a high quality "A7" size envelope. Finish the product by encasing in a clear plastic bag and price accordingly.

Chapter 14
AFTERWORD

REINVENTION

Polaroid imagery is appropriate for any application. Master the techniques presented here, then use them as springboards to new heights for your own work. Like all great techniques, any end result is solely dependent upon the quality of the original work. The soul of an image shines through any trick, no matter how well executed.

New techniques create new direction. Let your experiments with Polaroid imaging contribute to your success, personal or professional, as a photographer. If those experiments dominate your work for a while, that's fine. They just might reinvent your photographic ideals. When you apply what you've learned to other processes, who knows what the end result might be.

Always keep an open mind. An open checkbook won't hurt, either.

Good luck.

INDEX

Archiving, *see* Care and keeping
Black & white transfers, 9-11
Borderless prints, 47
Brayer, 13, 21, 29
Break lines, 53
Cameras, 85-86
Care and keeping, 90-92
  copying, 90-92
  fading, 90
Color transfers, 9
  manipulation of color, 49
  options, 9-10
Computers, *see* Digital technology
Digital technology, 97-99
  film recorder, 99
  Giclee prints, 97-98
  inkjet prints, 98
  Iris prints, 97
Dry transfers, 31-33
  imbibe time, 32
  flattening, 33
  materials needed, 31
  receptors, 31
  rolling, 33
Drying, 23, 47
Emulsion Lift-off, 57-66
  brightness, 70
  close-dated film, 69
  color, 67
  corners, 70
  drying, 58, 66
  finishing, 66
  heating, 61-66
  materials needed, 57
  mirror images, 71
  multiple images, 71
  outline images, 68, 74
  overall color, 67
  repairing holes, 69-70
  repositioning on color backgrounds, 67, 73
  sealing, 59
  trimming, 60
  wax paper, 63
Exposure, 45
  multiple, 88
  over/under exposure, 47
Film
  alkaline chemistry, 29
  close-dated, 69
  daylight balanced, 8
  expiration dates, 29
  history, 9
  pack, 8-9
  Pro 100, 11 (see also Transfers with Polacolor Pro 100)
  tungsten balanced, 8
  Type 57, 8
  Type 59, 8, 16, 31-32, 83-84
  Type 64T, 8, 16, 31-32, 83-84
  Type 79, 8, 16, 83-84
  Type 108, 8, 16, 31-32, 81
  Type 669, 8, 16, 31-32, 81

Type 679 , 8, 16, 81
Type 689, 8, 81
Type 809, 8, 16, 49, 84
types, 8-9
Filters
gels, 89
polarizing, 99
sepia, 10
soft focus, 5
warming, 10
Handcoloring, 55
Imbibe times, 15-20, 27-29, 32, 36, 45
Land, Dr. Edward, 7
Live transfers, 76, 85-89
Lysol, 28-29, 35, 52
Markets, 100-104
advertising, 101
editorial, 100
fine art, 103
portraiture, 101
wedding photography, 103
Microwave, 46-47
Multiple transfers, 51-52
Negative, 5, 16, 99
Overlapping transfers, 52
Photoshop, 93, 97
Polaroid transfer
defined, 5
history, 6-7
Positive, 5, 16
Posterization, 48
Printing techniques, 77-89
color corrections, 81
Daylab II slide printer, 77-79
Daylab Junior, 79-82
projection printing, 83-84
Receptors, 11-12, 31-33
adding color to, 53
heated, 24-26
preparation, 13-15
Reinvention, 105
Removing emulsion, 49
Roller, *see* Brayer
Sandpaper, 49
Scanning, *see* Digital technology
Skin tones, 47, 54
Slide printers, 87-89
Stop bath, 30
Texture, 49
adding over transfers, 49-50
adding under transfers, 49-50
Transfers with Polacolor Pro 100 material, 34-44
borders, 46
cleaning up the whites, 35
dry transfers, 35
hot iron process, 37-42
imbibe time, 36
Lysol, 35
overscrubbing, 37
treating water with an acid or base, 34
washing, 37
wet transfers, 34-41
Vignettes, 53
Wet transfers, 13-23
density shifts, 23
drying, 23
hairdryer, 27
heated carrier and receptor, 26
heated receptor, 24-25
imbibe time, 15-20
short, 27-29
Lysol, 28-29
materials needed, 13
preparation of receptor, 13-15
removing excess chemistry, 22
rolling, 21
safety, 15
special techniques, 24-30
separating receptor and carrier, 21-22, 29-30
stop bath, 30

Other Books from
Amherst Media, Inc.

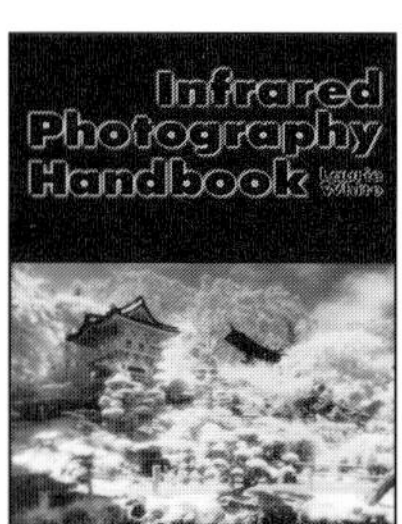

Infrared Photography Handbook

Laurie White

Covers b&w infrared photography: focus, lenses, film loading, film speed rating, heat sensitivity, batch testing, paper stocks, and filters. Photos illustrate IR film in portrait, landscape, and architectural photography. $29.95 list, 8½x11, 104p, 50 b&w photos, charts & diagrams, order no. 1419.

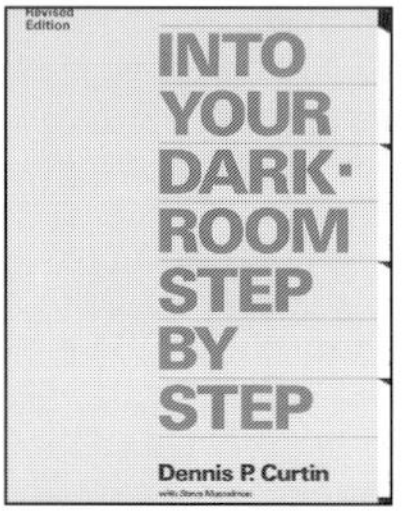

Into Your Darkroom Step-by-Step

Dennis P. Curtin

This is the ideal beginning darkroom guide. Easy to follow and fully illustrated each step of the way. Includes information on: the equipment you'll need, set-up, making proof sheets and much more! $17.95 list, 8½x11, 90p, hundreds of photos, order no. 1093.

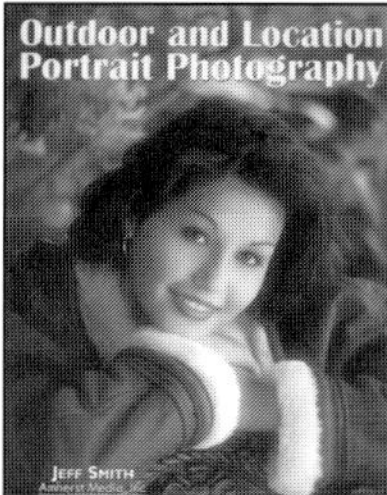

Outdoor and Location Portrait Photography

Jeff Smith

Learn how to work with natural light, select locations, and make clients look their best. Step-by-step discussions and helpful illustrations teach you the techniques you need to shoot outdoor portraits like a pro! $29.95 list, 8½x11, 128p, b&w and color photos, index, order no. 1632.

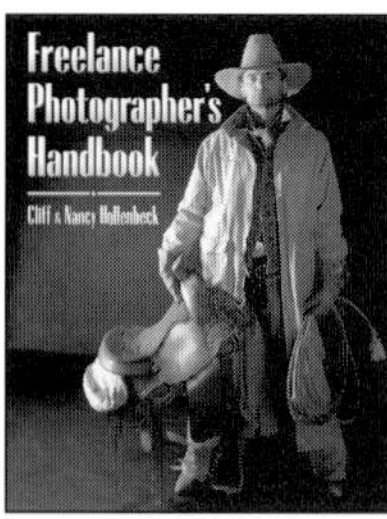

Freelance Photographer's Handbook

Cliff & Nancy Hollenbeck

Whether you want to be a freelance photographer or are looking for tips to improve your current freelance business, this volume is packed with ideas for creating and maintaining a successful freelance business. $29.95 list, 8½x11, 107p, 100 b&w and color photos, index, glossary, order no. 1633.

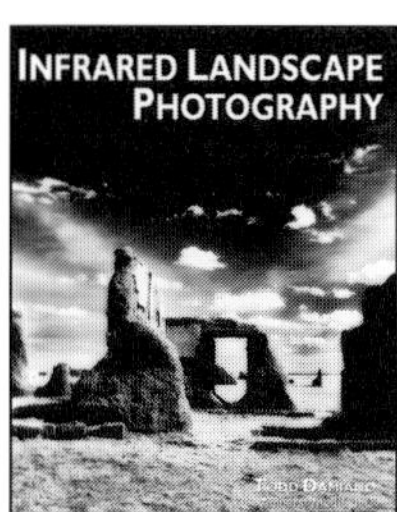

Infrared Landscape Photography

Todd Damiano

Landscapes shot with infrared can become breathtaking and ghostly images. The author analyzes over fifty of his most compelling photographs to teach you the techniques you need to capture landscapes with infrared. $29.95 list, 8½x11, 120p, b&w photos, index, order no. 1636.

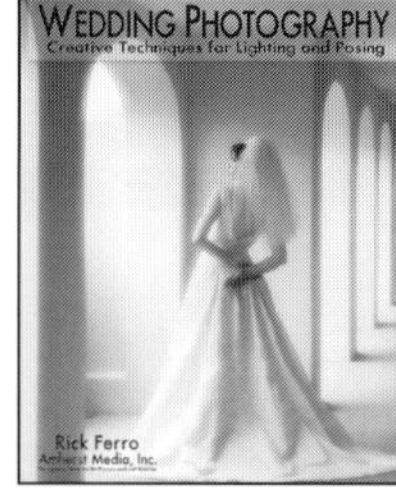

Wedding Photography: Creative Techniques for Lighting and Posing

Rick Ferro

Creative techniques for lighting and posing wedding portraits that will set your work apart from the competition. Covers every phase of wedding photography. $29.95 list, 8½x11, 128p, b&w and color photos, index, order no. 1649.

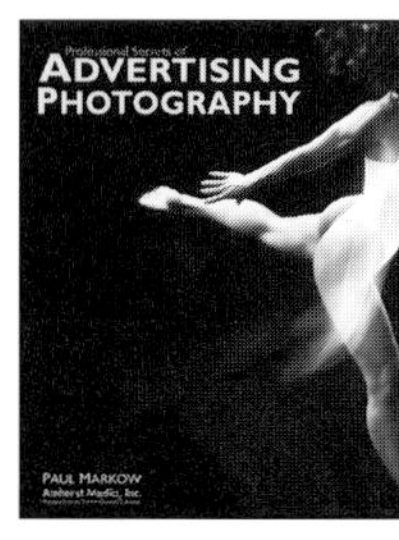

Professional Secrets of Advertising Photography

Paul Markow

No-nonsense information for those interested in the business of advertising photography. Includes: how to catch the attention of art directors, make the best bid, and produce the high-quality images your clients demand. $29.95 list, 8½x11, 128p, 80 photos, index, order no. 1638.

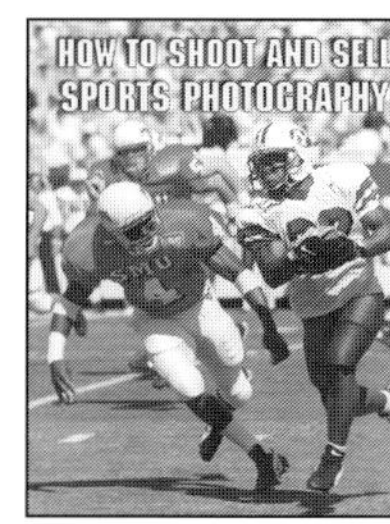

How to Shoot and Sell Sports Photography

David Arndt

A step-by-step guide for amateur photographers, photojournalism students and journalists seeking to develop the skills and knowledge necessary for success in the demanding field of sports photography. $29.95 list, 8½x11, 120p, 111 photos, index, order no. 1631.

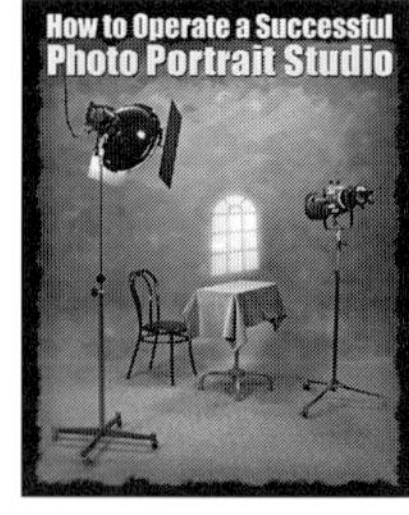

How to Operate a Successful Photo Portrait Studio

John Giolas

Combines photographic techniques with practical business information to create a complete guide book for anyone interested in developing a portrait photography business (or improving an existing business). $29.95 list, 8½x11, 120p, 120 photos, index, order no. 1579.

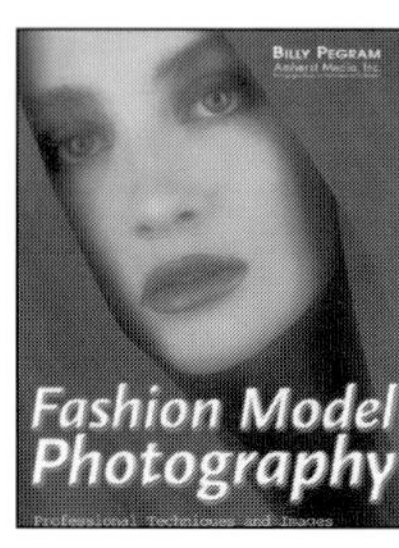

Fashion Model Photography

Billy Pegram

For the photographer interested in shooting commercial model assignments, or working with models to create portfolios. Includes techniques for dramatic composition, posing, selection of clothing, and more! $29.95 list, 8½x11, 120p, 58 photos, index, order no. 1640.

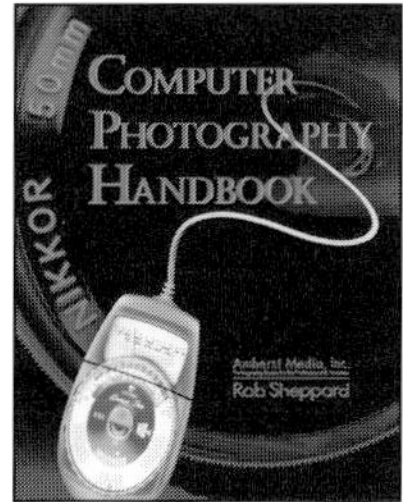

Computer Photography Handbook

Rob Sheppard

Learn to make the most of your photographs using computer technology! From creating images with digital cameras, to scanning prints and negatives, to manipulating images, you'll learn all the basics of digital imaging. $29.95 list, 8½x11, 128p, 150+ photos, index, order no. 1560.

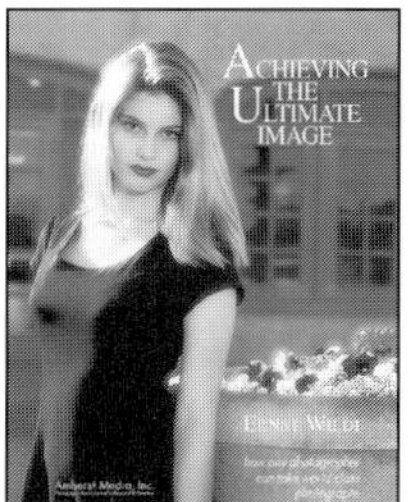

Achieving the Ultimate Image

Ernst Wildi

Ernst Wildi teaches the techniques required to take world class, technically flawless photos. Features: exposure, metering, the Zone System, composition, evaluating an image, and more! $29.95 list, 8½x11, 128p, 120 b&w and color photos, index, order no. 1628.

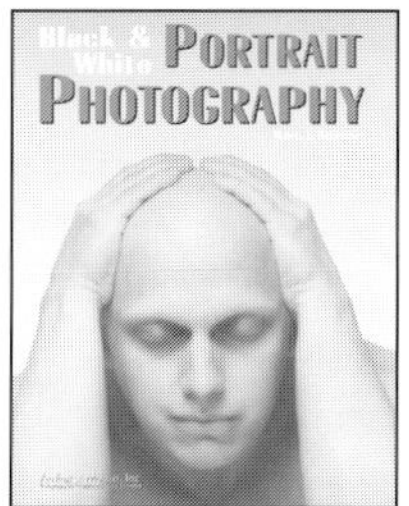

Black & White Portrait Photography

Helen Boursier

Make money with b&w portrait photography. Learn from top b&w shooters! Studio and location techniques, with tips on preparing your subjects, selecting settings and wardrobe, lab techniques, and more! $29.95 list, 8½x11, 128p, 130+ photos, index, order no. 1626

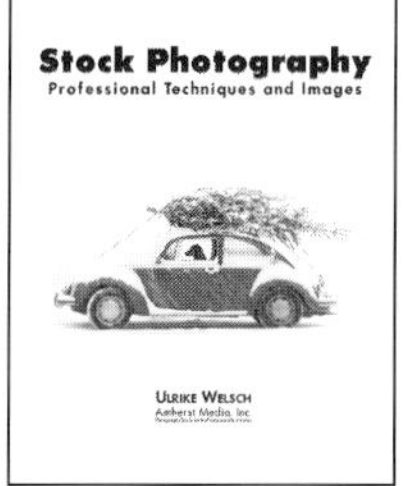

Stock Photography

Ulrike Welsh

This book provides an inside look at the business of stock photography. Explore photographic techniques and business methods that will lead to success shooting stock photos — creating both excellent images and business opportunities. $29.95 list, 8½x11, 120p, 58 photos, index, order no. 1634.

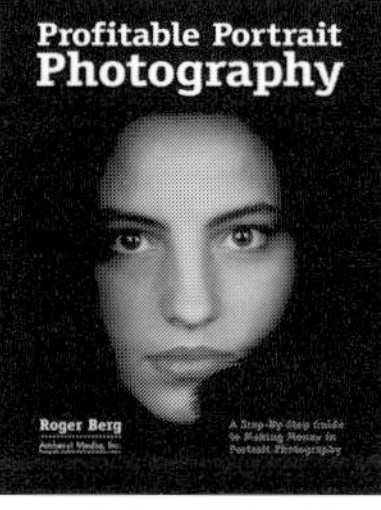

Profitable Portrait Photography

Roger Berg

A step-by-step guide to making money in portrait photography. Combines information on portrait photography with detailed business plans to form a comprehensive manual for starting or improving your business. $29.95 list, 81/2x11, 104p, 100 photos, index, order no. 1570

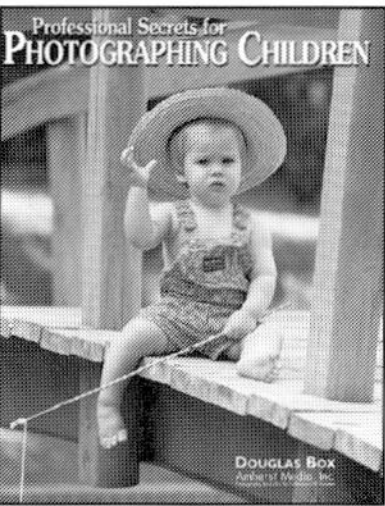

Professional Secrets for Photographing Children

Douglas Allen Box

Covers every aspect of photographing children on location and in the studio. Prepare children and parents for the shoot, select the right clothes capture a child's personality, and shoot story book themes. $29.95 list, 8½x11, 128p, 74 photos, index, order no. 1635.

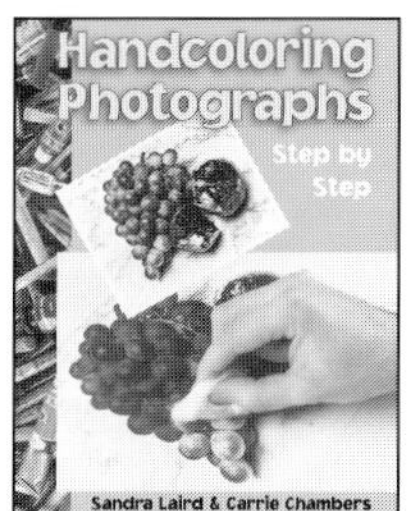

Handcoloring Photographs Step-by-Step

Sandra Laird & Carey Chambers

Learn to handcolor photographs step-by-step with the new standard in handcoloring reference books. Covers a variety of coloring media and techniques with plenty of colorful photographic examples. $29.95 list, 8½x11, 112p, 100+ color and b&w photos, index, order no. 1543.

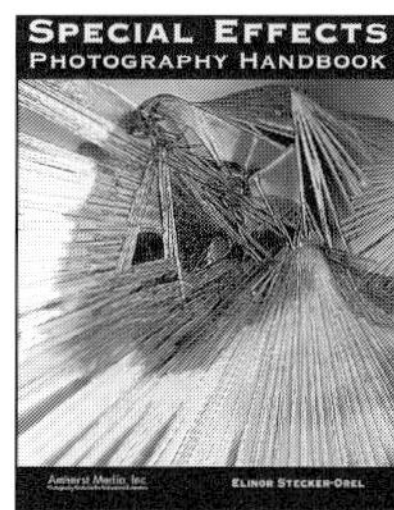

Special Effects Photography Handbook

Elinor Stecker Orel

Create magic on film with special effects! Little or no additional equipment required, use things you probably have around the house. Step-by-step instructions guide you through each effect. $29.95 list, 8½x11, 112p, 80+ color and b&w photos, index, glossary, order no. 1614.

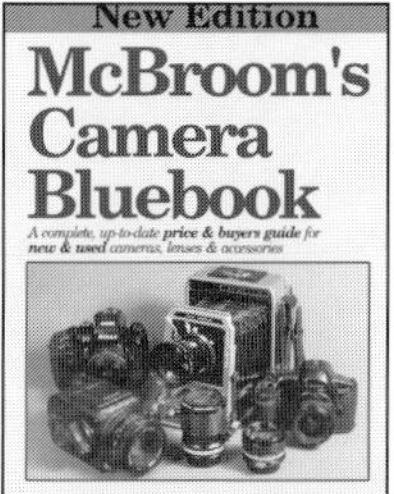

McBroom's Camera Bluebook

Mike McBroom

Comprehensive and fully illustrated, with price information on: 35mm, medium & large format cameras, exposure meters, strobes and accessories. Pricing info based on equipment condition. A must for any camera buyer, dealer, or collector! $29.95 list, 8½x11, 224p, 75+ photos, order no. 1263.

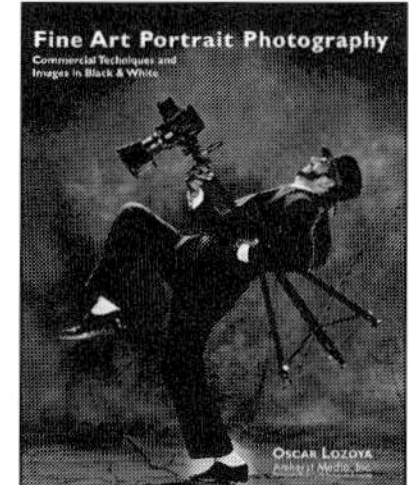

Fine Art Portrait Photography

Oscar Lozoya

The author examines a selection of his best photographs, and provides detailed technical information about how he created each. Lighting diagrams accompany each photograph. $29.95 list, 8½x11, 128p, 58 photos, index, order no. 1630.

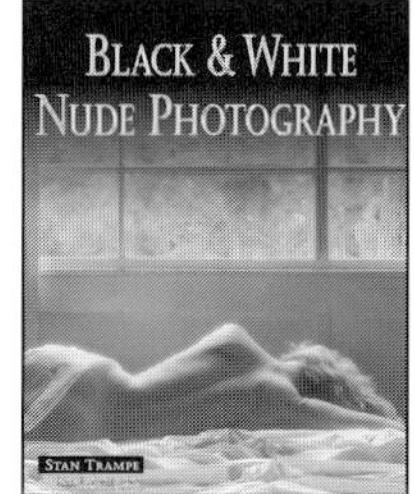

Black & White Nude Photography

Stan Trampe

This book teaches the essentials for beginning fine art nude photography. Includes info on finding your first model, selecting equipment, and scenarios of a typical shoot, plus more! Includes 60 photos taken with b&w and infrared films. $24.95 list, 8½x11, 112p, index, order no. 1592.

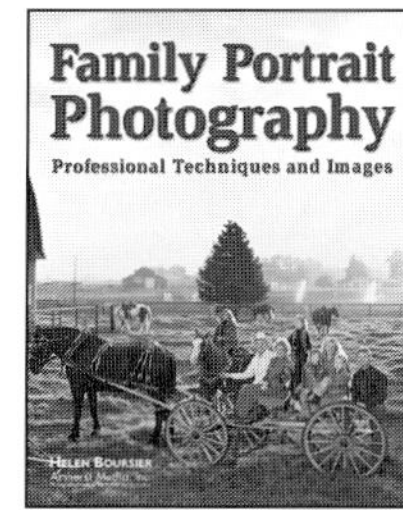

Family Portrait Photography

Helen Boursier

Learn from professionals how to operate a successful portrait studio. Includes: marketing family portraits, advertising, working with clients, posing, lighting, and selection of equipment. Includes images from a variety of top portrait shooters. $29.95 list, 8½x11, 120p, 123 photos, index, order no. 1629.

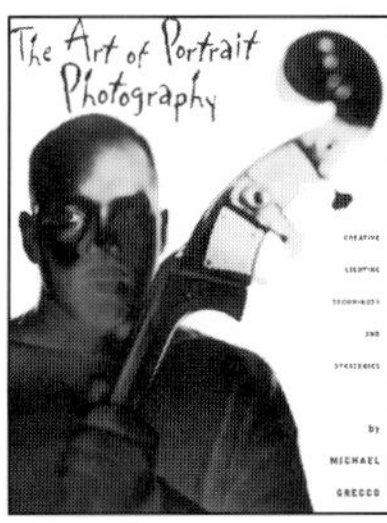

The Art of Portrait Photography

Michael Grecco

Michael Grecco reveals the secrets behind his dramatic portraits which have appeared in magazines such as *Rolling Stone* and *Entertainment Weekly*. Includes: lighting, posing, creative development, and more! $29.95 list, 8½x11, 128p, order no. 1651.

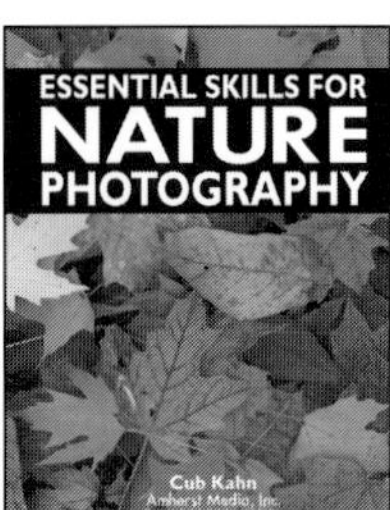

Essential Skills for Nature Photography

Cub Kahn

Learn all the skills you need to capture landscapes, animals, flowers and the entire natural world on film. Includes: selecting equipment, choosing locations, evaluating compositions, filters, and much more! $29.95 list, 8½x11, 128p, order no. 1652.

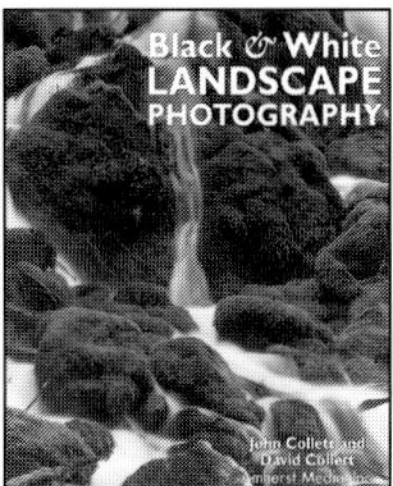

Black & White Landscape Photography

John Collett and David Collett

Master the art of b&w landscape photography. Includes: selecting equipment (cameras, lenses, filters, etc.) for landscape photography, shooting in the field, using the Zone System, and printing your images for professional results. $29.95 list, 8½x11, 128p, order no. 1654.

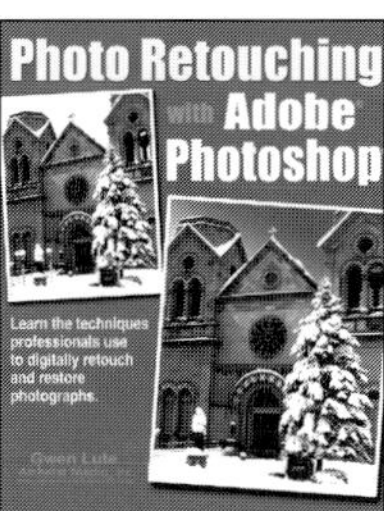

Photo Retouching with Adobe Photoshop

Gwen Lute

Designed for photographers, this manual teaches every phase of the process, from scanning to final output. Learn to restore damaged photos, correct imperfections, create realistic composite images and correct for dazzling color. $29.95 list, 8½x11, 128p, order no. 1660.

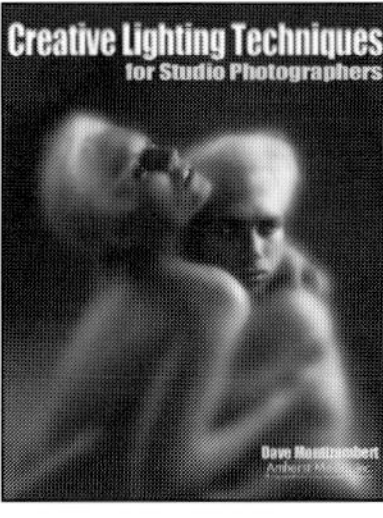

Creative Lighting Techniques for Studio Photographers

Dave Montizambert

Master studio lighting and gain complete creative control over your images. Whether you are shooting portraits, cars, table-top or any other subject, Dave Montizambert teaches you the skills you need to confidently create with light. $29.95 list, 8½x11, 128p, order]
no. 1666.

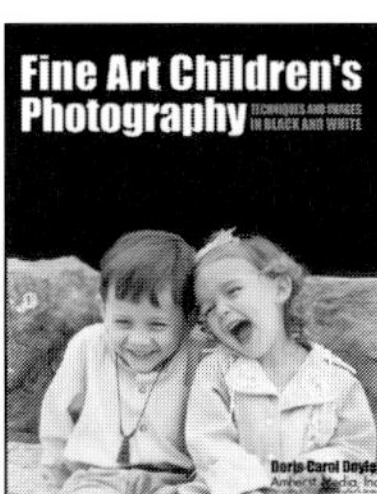

Fine Art Children's Photography

Doris Carol Doyle

Learn to create fine art portraits of children in black & white. Included is information on: posing, lighting for studio portraits, shooting on location, clothing selection, working with kids and parents, and much more! $29.95 list, 8½x11, 128p, order no. 1668.

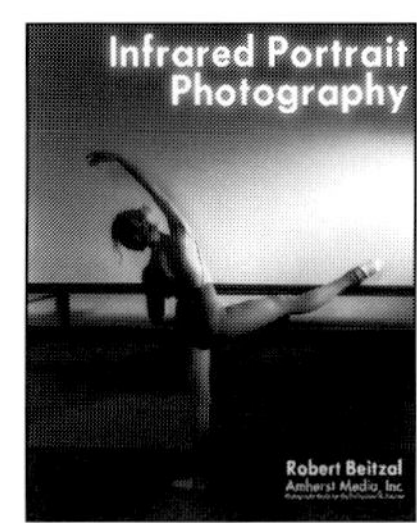

Infrared Portrait Photography

Richard Beitzel

Discover the unique beauty of infrared portraits, and learn to create them yourself. Included is information on: shooting with infrared, selecting subjects and settings, filtration, lighting, and much more! $29.95 list, 8½x11, 128p, order no. 1669.

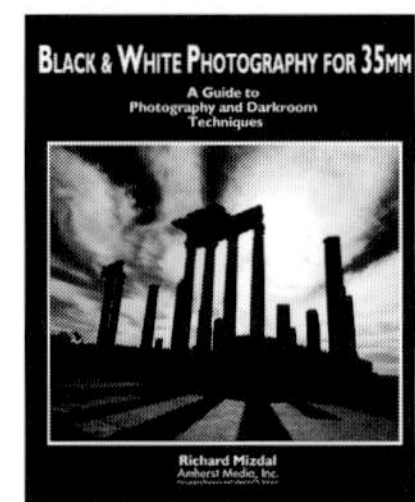

Black & White Photography for 35mm

Richard Mizdal

A guide to shooting and darkroom techniques! Perfect for beginning or intermediate photo-graphers who wants to improve their skills. Features helpful illustrations and exercises to make every concept clear and easy to follow. $29.95 list, 8½x11, 128p, order no. 1670.

More Photo Books Are Available!

Write or fax for a *FREE* catalog:

AMHERST MEDIA, INC.
PO BOX 586
AMHERST, NY 14226 USA

Fax: 716-874-4508

Ordering & Sales Information:

INDIVIDUALS: If possible, purchase books from an Amherst Media retailer. Write to us for the dealer nearest you. To order direct, send a check or money order with a note listing the books you want and your shipping address. U.S. & overseas freight charges are $3.50 first book and $1.00 for each additional book. Visa and Master Card accepted. New York state residents add 8% sales tax.

DEALERS, DISTRIBUTORS & COLLEGES: Write, call or fax to place orders. For price information, contact Amherst Media or an Amherst Media sales representative. Net 30 days.

All prices, publication dates, and specifications are subject to change without notice.

Prices are in U.S. dollars. Payment in U.S. funds only.

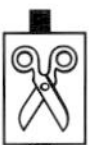

cut along dotted line

Amherst Media's Customer Registration Form

Please fill out this sheet and send or fax to receive free information about future publications from Amherst Media.

Customer Information

Date

Name

Street or Box #

City State

Zip Code

Phone ( ) Fax ( )

Optional Information

I bought *Photographer's Guide to Polaroid Transfer* because

I found these chapters to be most useful

I purchased the book from

City State

I would like to see more books about

I purchase books per year

Additional comments

FAX to: 1-800-622-3298

if mailing, fold in number order along dashed lines.

①

②

Name______________________________
Address____________________________
City____________________State_____
Zip________________ — ________

Place
Postage
Here

Amherst Media, Inc.
PO Box 586
Buffalo, NY 14226

③

if mailing, paste underside of flap, or tape here.